Virginia's

Forests, 2007

Anita K. Rose

United States
Department of
Agriculture

Forest Service

Southern
Research Station

Resource Bulletin
SRS-159

Anita K. Rose is an Ecologist with the U.S. Department of Agriculture Forest Service, Southern Research Station, Forest Inventory and Analysis Research Work Unit, Knoxville, TN 37919.

Front cover: top left, oaks and maples in fall colors line Minton Lane, Lee County, VA. (photo by Harold Jerrell, Lee County, VA, Virginia Cooperative Extension); top right, view from Pinnacle Overlook, Cumberland Gap National Historic Park, Lee County, VA. (photo by Harold Jerrell, Lee County, VA, Virginia Cooperative Extension); bottom, maidenhair fern. (photo by Anita K. Rose). Back cover: top left, Keokee Lake near Appalachia in Lee County, VA. (photo by Harold Jerrell, Lee County, VA, Virginia Cooperative Extension); top right, oaks and maples in fall colors line Minton Lane, Lee County, VA. (photo by Harold Jerrell, Lee County, VA, Virginia Cooperative Extension); bottom, ruffed grouse, Cumberland Mountain, Lee County, VA (photo by Harold Jerrell, Lee County, VA, Virginia Cooperative Extension)

Spotted mandarin, Natural Tunnel State Park, Scott County, VA. (photo by Harold Jerrell, Lee County, VA, Virginia Cooperative Extension)

Virginia's
Forests, 2007

Anita K. Rose

Oaks and maples in fall colors line Minton Lane, Lee County, VA. (photo by Harold Jerrell, Lee County, VA, Virginia Cooperative Extension)

About Forest Inventory and Analysis Inventory Reports

The Forest Service, U.S. Department of Agriculture, Southern Research Station's Forest Inventory and Analysis (FIA) Research Work Unit and cooperating State forestry agencies conduct annual forest inventories of resources in the 13 Southern States (Alabama, Arkansas, Florida, Georgia, Kentucky, Louisiana, Mississippi, North Carolina, Oklahoma, South Carolina, Tennessee, Texas, and Virginia), the Commonwealth of Puerto Rico, and the U.S. Virgin Islands. In order to provide more frequent and nationally consistent information on America's forest resources, all research stations and work units conduct annual surveys, which are mandated by the Agricultural Research Extension and Education Reform Act of 1998 (Farm Bill).

The primary objective in conducting these inventories is to gather the resource information needed to formulate sound forest policies and programs. These data are analyzed to provide a view of forest resources including, but not limited to, forest area, forest ownership, forest type, stand structure, timber volume, growth, removals, and management activity. In addition, assessments that help address issues of ecosystem health include information about ozone-induced injury, down woody material, soils, lichens, and tree crown condition. The information presented is applicable at the State and unit level; it furnishes the background for intensive studies of critical situations but is not designed to reflect resource conditions at very small scales.

View from Pinnacle Overlook, Cumberland Gap National Historic Park, Lee County, VA. (photo by Harold Jerrell, Lee County, VA, Virginia Cooperative Extension)

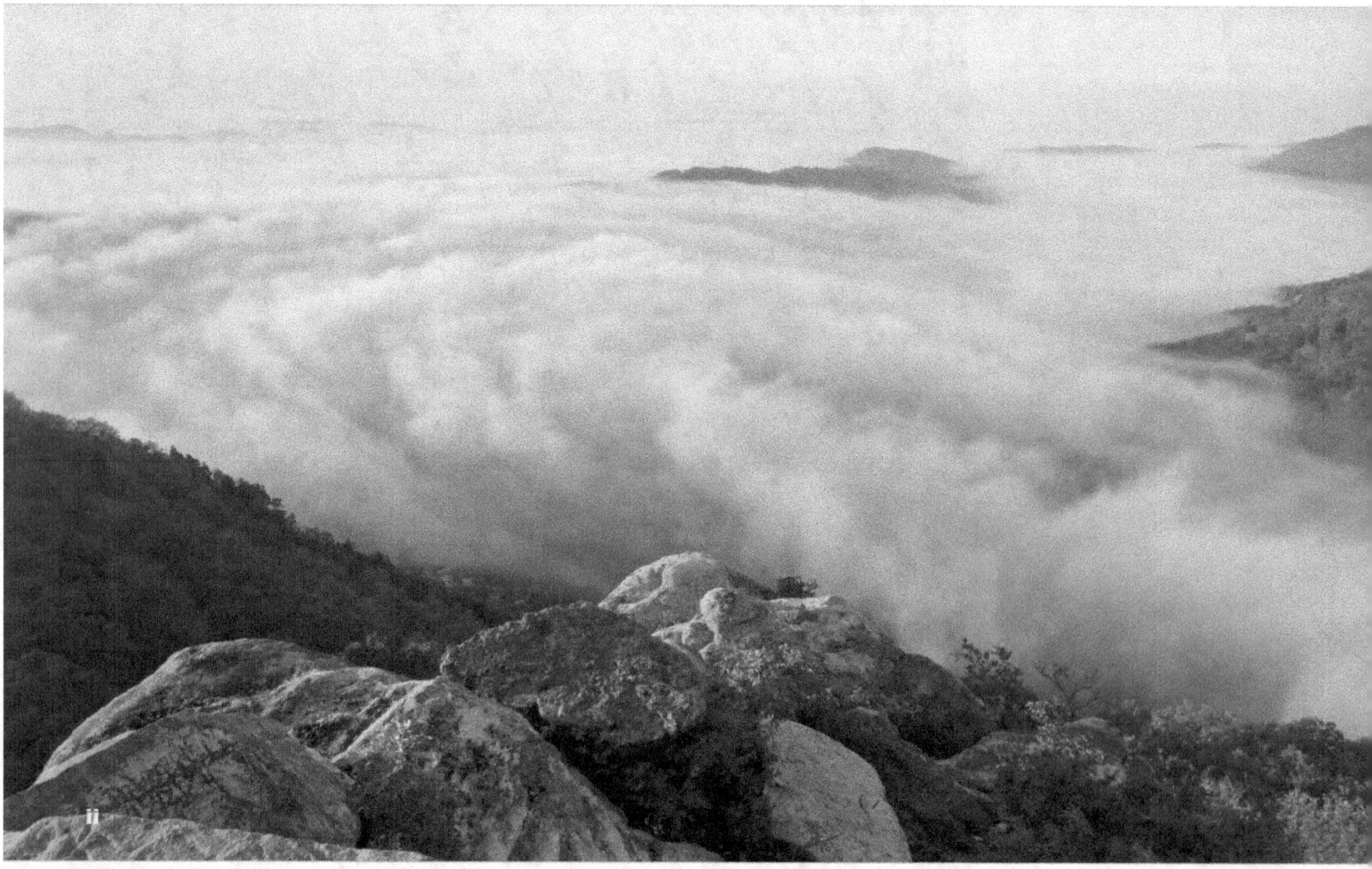

More information about Forest Service resource inventories is available in "Forest Service Resource Inventories: An Overview" (U.S. Department of Agriculture Forest Service 1992). More detailed information about sampling methodologies used in the annual FIA inventories can be found in "The Enhanced Forest Inventory and Analysis Program—National Sampling Design and Estimation Procedures" (Bechtold and Patterson 2005).

Data tables included in FIA reports are designed to provide an array of forest resource estimates, but additional tables can be obtained at http://srsfia2.fs.fed. us/states/virginia.shtml. For those who require more specialized information, FIA data for all States are retrievable at http:// fia.fs.fed.us/tools-data/default.asp.

Additional information about any aspect of this or other FIA surveys may be obtained from:

Forest Inventory and Analysis
Southern Research Station
4700 Old Kingston Pike
Knoxville, TN 37919

Telephone: 865-862-2000

William G. Burkman
Program Manager

Acknowledgments

FIA thanks the Virginia Department of Forestry for partnering with our program in conducting data collection for the survey that the author reports here. FIA also thanks other public agencies and the many private landowners who provided access to measurement plots.

The following people made field measurements for this survey. FIA appreciates their hard work and their consistent efforts to obtain high-quality data.

Virginia Department of Forestry

Trent Badgley
Justin Barnes
Onesphore Bitoki
Joseph Blaylock
Thomas Callahan
Cesar Carrion
Scarlet Collie
Justin Funk
Thomas Furcron
Douglas Godbee
Steve Grayson
Jeffrey Grieco

Amy Haynes
G.T. Hughes
Mason Jeffries
Sarah Kendig
Porter Knight
Shannon Lewis
Bryan Litchfield
Jean Lorber
Chad Lykins
Tracy McDonald
Matthew Monaghan
Lou Murray
Neale Nickels
Paul Owen
Ben Parsons
John Pemberton
Winston Percefull
Lynwood Rogers
Joe Rossetti
Kyla Sabo
Michael Salyer
John Scrivani
Scott Siebert
Tom Snoddy
Randall Stamper
Mark Webb
Paul Whitehead III

Forest Service

Chris Brown
Benjamin Koontz
Lucas Recore

Azalea, Nelson County, VA.
(photo by Anita K. Rose)

Contents

Contents

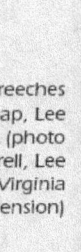

Dutchman's breeches at Lovelady Gap, Lee County, VA. (photo by Harold Jerrell, Lee County, VA, Virginia Cooperative Extension)

List of Figures

Text Figures

Appendix Figure

Page

Text Tables

The Powell River, seen here at Beech Grove, flows through Lee and Wise County, VA.
(photo by Harold Jerrell, Lee County, VA, Virginia Cooperative Extension)

Page

Appendix Tables

• In 2007, about 15.7 million acres, or 62 percent, of Virginia's land area was forested. This was a slight decrease from the 2001 suvey, when forest land totaled 15.8 million acres.

• Most (12.4 million acres) of Virginia's forest land was in nonindustrial private forest (NIPF) ownership, which increased by 2.3 percent since 2001. Public ownership ranked second with 2.8 million acres (18 percent). Forest industry owned 3.5 percent, or 551,200 acres, of forest land across the State, a decrease of 46 percent.

• The predominant forest-type group in Virginia was oak-hickory. It occupied 62 percent, or 9.8 million acres, of forest land area and contained 65 percent (21.4 billion cubic feet) of the live volume across the State. Loblolly-shortleaf was the second most dominant forest-type group in both area (3.0 million acres) and volume (5.5 billion cubic feet). The oak-pine forest-type group ranked third, occupying 1.6 million acres.

• Most of Virginia's forest land was in sawtimber- and poletimber-sized stands, 9.6 million acres (61 percent) and 3.6 million acres (23 percent), respectively. Sapling-seedling-sized stands occupied 15 percent and nonstocked stands occupied 1 percent of forest land.

• Volume of live trees ≥ 5.0 inches diameter at breast height increased from 31.5 to 32.8 billion cubic feet. Softwoods made up 23 percent of the live volume and hardwoods 77 percent.

• Yellow-poplar continued to dominate the State's live-tree volume with 5.0 billion cubic feet, an increase of 9 percent since 2001. Red maple was dominant in terms of live stems, constituting 1.4 billion stems.

White Branch near Rose Hill, VA. (photo by Harold Jerrell, Lee County, VA, Virginia Cooperative Extension)

• Net annual growth for all live trees on timberland for the 2007 survey period was 1,030.4 million cubic feet per year, an increase of 4.1 percent over the previous survey period. Since 2001, Virginia's live-tree removals averaged 827.5 million cubic feet per year. This was an increase of 19 percent over the previous survey period. Growth exceeded removals in all units except the Coastal Plain, the area most impacted by Hurricane Isabel.

• Japanese honeysuckle, nonnative roses, and tree-of-heaven were the most often occurring invasive species in Virginia's forests.

• Only 22 percent of phase 3 (P3) plots in Virginia had soil compaction on more than 5 percent of the plot area. The majority of mineral soil samples had a pH < 5.1. The mineral soil accounted for 16.8 tons per acre of organic carbon.

• The biomass of coarse woody debris (CWD) on P3 plots averaged 2.9 tons per acre for the State. The amount of carbon in CWD and fine woody debris averaged 1.4 and 1.7 tons per acre, respectively.

The Virginia State champion shagbark hickory, which is just over 43 inches d.b.h., is in Lee county, VA.
(photo by Harold Jerrell, Lee County, VA, Virginia Cooperative Extension)

Introduction

Field measurements for this inventory of Virginia's forests began in February 2002 and were completed in August 2007. Even though measurements were spread over several years, the survey is dated 2007. Comparisons, unless otherwise noted, are based on estimates from the 2001 and the 2007 surveys. The seven previous surveys and State analytical reports were completed in 1940 (Craig 1949), 1957 (Larson and Bryan 1959), 1966 (Knight and McClure 1967), 1977 (Knight and McClure 1978), 1986 (Bechtold and others 1987), 1992 (Thompson and Johnson 1994), and 2001 (Rose 2007). Numerous other publications were developed using those surveys.

With a total of 25.3 million acres of land, Virginia includes a variety of physiographic provinces (fig. 1). The Appalachian Plateaus form the western border with North Carolina and are composed of the eastern escarpment of the Cumberland and Allegheny Mountains. To the east of these mountains are the Ridge and Valley Province and the Blue Ridge Mountains.

Keokee Lake near Appalachia in Lee County, VA. (photo by Harold Jerrell, Lee County, VA, Virginia Cooperative Extension)

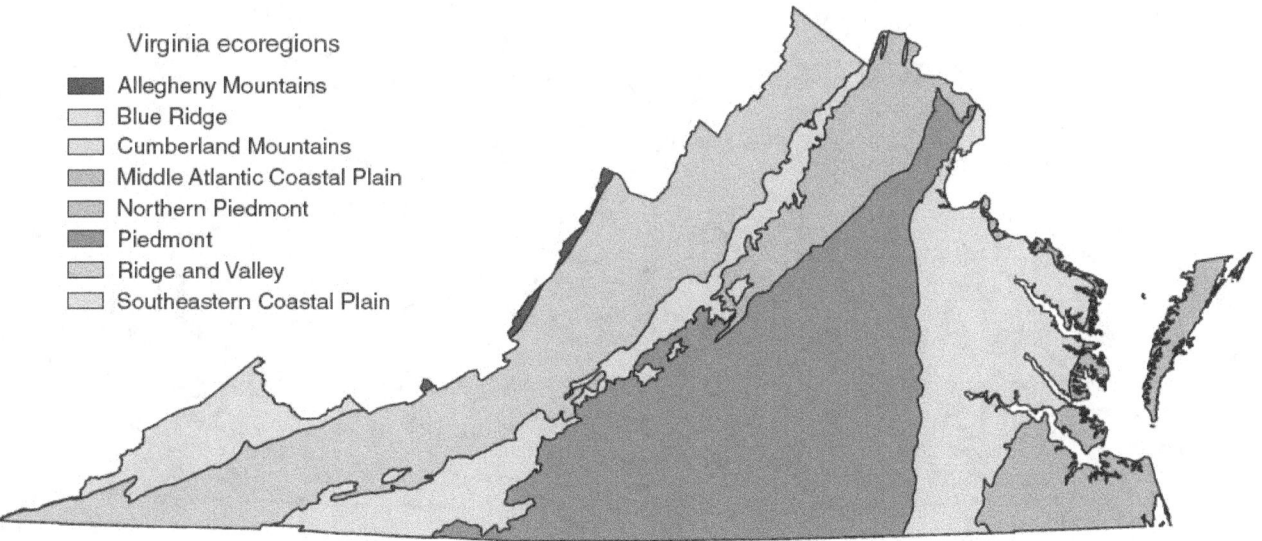

Virginia ecoregions

- Allegheny Mountains
- Blue Ridge
- Cumberland Mountains
- Middle Atlantic Coastal Plain
- Northern Piedmont
- Piedmont
- Ridge and Valley
- Southeastern Coastal Plain

Figure 1—Physiographic provinces in Virginia.

View from Powell Mountain overlook near Duffield, VA. (photo by Harold Jerrell, Lee County, VA, Virginia Cooperative Extension)

Further east is the Piedmont, which ranges from rolling hills in the west to several nearly level basins in the east. The easternmost part of the State is on the Coastal Plain, which extends inland approximately 125 miles from the coast and about the same distance from the Potomac to the southern boundary. The Coastal Plain is defined by the eastern Atlantic shore and the rolling and dissected area where it meets the Piedmont at the fall line (Fenneman 1938). The State's elevation ranges from sea level to just over 5,700 feet on Mount Rogers in the George Washington and Jefferson National Forests. For the purposes of this report Virginia is divided into five survey units that approximate the physiographic provinces found in the State. These units are the Coastal Plain, Southern Piedmont, Northern Piedmont, Northern Mountains, and Southern Mountains (fig. 2).

Figure 2—Counties and forest survey units in Virginia. (Note: Boundaries for the 37 independent cities that FIA includes within a larger county, because of their unusually small size, have been omitted. For example, Portsmouth (City) County is included within Chesapeake County and its boundaries are not shown on this map.)

Forest Area

Trends in Forest Area

In 2007, about 15.7 million acres, or 62 percent, of Virginia's land area was forested (table 1). Of this total, 15.2 million acres were classified as timberland. About 406,100 acres were classified as reserved timberland; this includes such areas as wilderness, parks, and historic sites—where commercial timber harvesting is prohibited by statute. The remaining 75,500 acres were classified as other forest land, land that, because of adverse site conditions, cannot produce at least 20 cubic feet of wood per acre per year.

Natural forest reversion near Galax, VA, a common scene on the Piedmont. (photo by Anita K. Rose)

Table 1—Area of forest land by survey year, unit, and ownership class, Virginia

Survey year and unit	Ownership class				
	All classes	National forests	Other public	Forest industry	Nonindustrial private
			thousand acres		
2001					
Coastal Plain	3,817.7	—	293.0	418.0	3,106.6
Southern Piedmont	3,784.1	18.3	195.5	302.0	3,268.3
Northern Piedmont	2,405.1	85.7	267.2	110.5	1,941.7
Northern Mountains	2,744.3	1,102.3	181.4	71.9	1,388.7
Southern Mountains	3,092.9	486.0	88.6	121.8	2,396.6
All units	15,844.0	1,692.2	1,025.7	1,024.2	12,101.9
2007					
Coastal Plain	3,701.0	—	317.3	240.5	3,143.3
Southern Piedmont	3,741.7	22.0	188.4	146.2	3,385.1
Northern Piedmont	2,502.9	71.4	255.5	58.4	2,117.5
Northern Mountains	2,713.5	1,124.3	186.3	23.4	1,379.5
Southern Mountains	3,065.6	531.7	101.4	82.6	2,349.8
All units	15,724.8	1,749.5	1,048.9	551.2	12,375.3

Numbers in rows and columns may not sum to totals due to rounding.
— = no sample for the cell.

Proportionally, the Southern Piedmont was the most heavily forested (at 67 percent), and the Northern Piedmont the least (at 57 percent). Since 2001, forest area decreased by < 1 percent across the State (fig. 3). Agricultural and urban/developed land uses dominated Virginia's nonforest land. In 2007, about 5.6 million acres were in agriculture and 3.5 million acres were

considered urban or developed. The change in forest area since 2001 represented both reversions from nonforest and diversions to nonforest. About 3 percent of forest land was diverted to nonforest (just under 500,000 acres), however, about three-fourths of that was replaced by reversions. Sixty-two percent of the gain in forest land came from the reversion of agricultural land. The reversion of agricultural land is a continuing trend that is reflected in the first survey of Virginia. Thirty percent of the diversions of forest land were to agriculture, and 63 percent were losses to urban development and other nonagricultural land uses.

Ownership

Just over three-fourths (12.4 million acres) of Virginia's forest land was held in nonindustrial private forest (NIPF) ownership, an increase of 2.3 percent from 2001 to 2007. Public ownership ranked second with 2.8 million acres (18 percent). The National Forest System owned 1.7 million acres of public lands across the

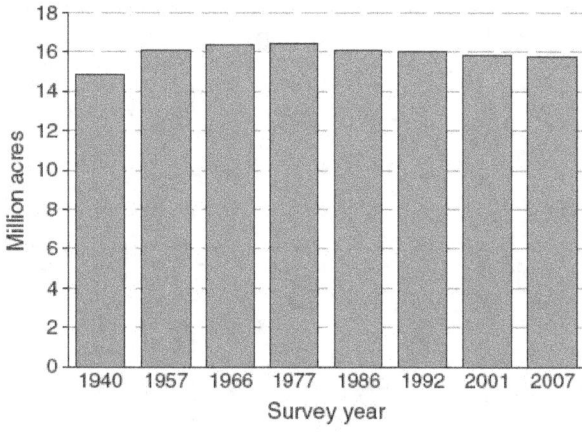

Figure 3—Area of forest land by survey year, Virginia.

View from Lover's Leap, Patrick County, near Vesta, VA. This shows typical heavily forested slopes and farming in the valleys. (photo by Anita K. Rose)

State, with the George Washington and Jefferson National Forests accounting for most of that total. Other public lands include the Shenandoah National Park, the Great Dismal Swamp National Wildlife Refuge, Marine Corps Base Quantico, Fort A.P. Hill and Fort Pickett Military Facilities, as well as State forests and parks. Forest industry owned 3.5 percent, or 551,200 acres, of forest land across the State. This was a decrease of 46 percent since 2001, continuing a trend that began in the mid-1980s. This trend is not unique to Virginia, however; it has been noted throughout the South.

Because so much of the forest land in the United States is privately owned, the Forest Service enhanced the assessment of ownership characteristics with an improved National Woodland Owner Survey (NWOS) in 2002. The primary goals of the NWOS are to determine who owns forest lands in the United States, why people own forest lands, and how those owners intend to use forest lands in the future (Butler and others 2005). Two key functions the NWOS

serves are to facilitate the planning and implementation of forest policies, and to support forest sustainability assessments in the United States.

While most (89 percent) private forest land owners have < 50 acres, the majority (67 percent) of the forest land acreage is controlled by only 11 percent of private owners (fig. 4). This means that a small

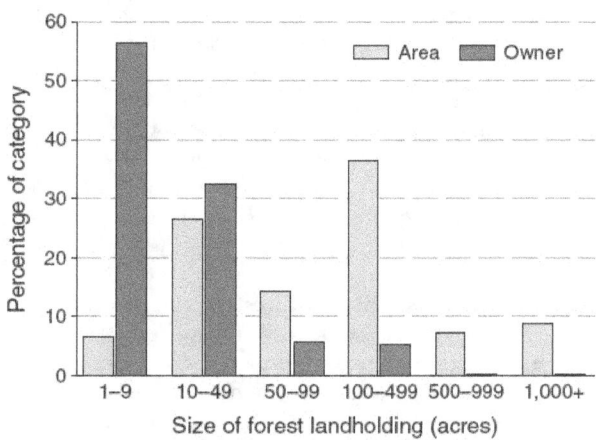

Figure 4—Percentage of area and private forest land owners by size of forest landholding, National Woodland Owner Survey, Virginia, 2007.

Marsh opening on Jamestown Island Colonial National Historic Park. (photo by Anita K. Rose)

number of private owners with large landholdings control the majority of land that potentially may be available for timber harvesting.

Forest-Type Groups

As would be expected in a State with an area of 25.3 million acres and elevations ranging from sea level to just under 6,000 feet, Virginia's forests contained a wide variety of tree species. These species occur in associations known as forest types. Some forest types occurred across the entire State, while others were restricted to limited areas especially suitable for particular species. Similar forest types are aggregated into forest-type groups.

The predominant forest-type group in Virginia was oak-hickory. It occupied 62 percent, or 9.8 million acres, of the forest land area and contained 65 percent (21.4 billion cubic feet) of the live volume across the State (figs. 5 and 6). In 2001, this

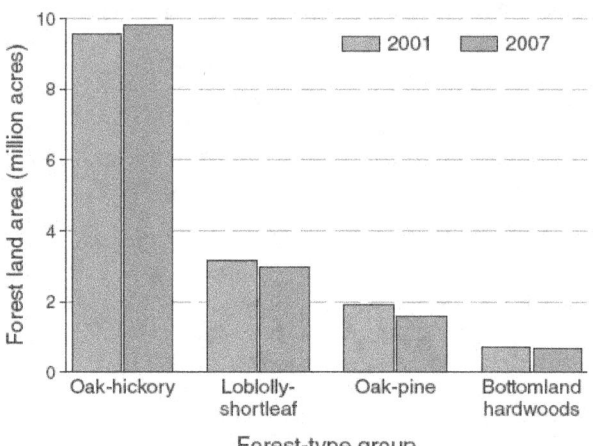

Figure 5—Area of forest land by survey year and forest-type group, Virginia.

forest-type group occupied 60 percent, or 9.5 million acres, of the forest land area and contained 64 percent (20.1 billion cubic feet) of the live volume across the State. Loblolly-shortleaf was the second most dominant forest-type group in both area and volume. In 2007 it occupied 3.0 million acres (19 percent) of the State's forest land,

Table Mountain Pine in the candle stage, Patrick County, VA. (photo by Anita K. Rose)

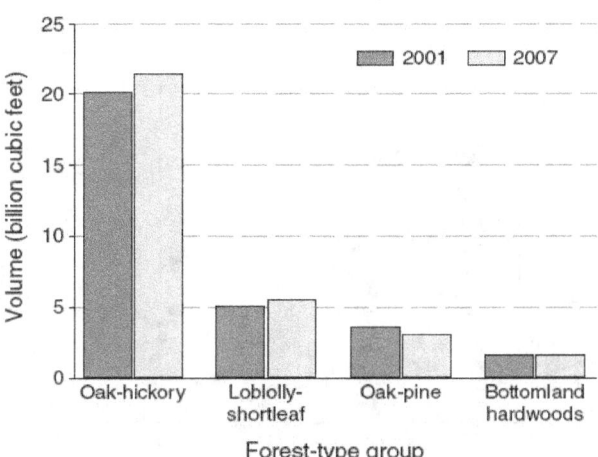

Figure 6—Volume of live trees on forest land by survey year and forest-type group, Virginia.

and contained 5.5 billion cubic feet (17 percent) of the live volume. This was both a decrease in area and an increase in volume from 2001, when this forest-type group occupied 3.2 million acres (20 percent) of the State's forest land area and contained 5.1 billion cubic feet (16 percent) of the live volume. Natural loblolly-shortleaf stands accounted for the majority of the loss in area, while planted stands accounted for all of the increase in volume in this forest-type group. The oak-pine forest-type group, which ranked third, decreased from 1.9 million to 1.6 million acres, and from 3.6 billion to 3.1 billion cubic feet of live volume. Between 7 and 25 percent of each of the five major forest-type groups was in public ownership. Nearly 50 percent of forest-industry owned land was in the loblolly-shortleaf forest-type group.

Stand Size

In 2007, 61 percent (9.6 million acres) of Virginia's forest land was in the sawtimber stand-size class, and 23 percent (3.6 million acres) was in the poletimber stand-size class. The sapling-seedling stands constituted an additional 15 percent of forest land area. Virginia was comparable to other Southern States in percentage of forest land area in sawtimber. For example, both Tennessee and Kentucky had 65 percent of their forest land in sawtimber (fig. 7) (Miles 2008). Nearly 75 percent of stands in public ownership were in the sawtimber-size class, while only 42 percent of those on forest industry land were in that class. In addition, 67 percent of natural stands were in the sawtimber-size class, while only 30 percent of planted stands were. This is not surprising, though, because 97 percent of public forest land was natural stands, while nearly 50 percent of forest industry land was artificially regenerated—reflecting management practices that are common on such lands.

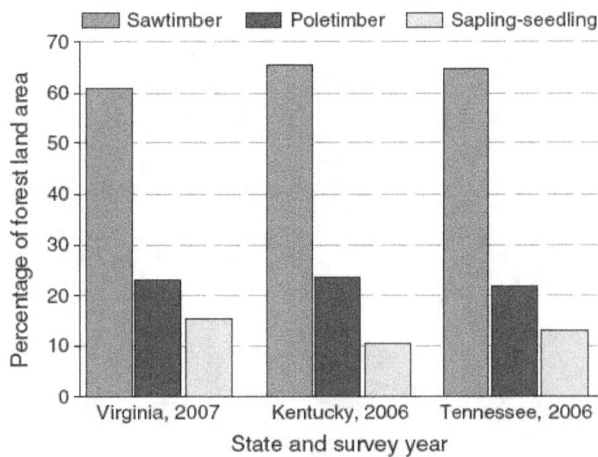

Figure 7—Percentage of forest land area by stand size, State, and survey year.

Stand Age

Stands 0 to 20 years old and those 61 to 80 years old accounted for 23 percent of forest land, each. Fifty-eight percent, or 9.2 million acres, of Virginia's forest land was > 40 years old, while 17 percent was > 80 years old. Acreage on forest industry lands, which is usually managed more intensively than forest land in other ownership categories, was primarily in young stands. Forest industry led all ownership categories with 68 percent of forest land in stands ≤ 40 years old, while public lands had the smallest fraction (16 percent) of their forest land in those age classes (fig. 8). Public lands had 71 percent of their forest land in stands > 60 years old while forest industry had the smallest proportion of its forest land in stands > 60 years old (18 percent). This may in part be due to the shortness of rotation lengths on forest industry lands. For example, if the rotation length of a pine plantation is 25 years, then the plantation will spend 80 percent of its life in the 0- to 20-year age class.

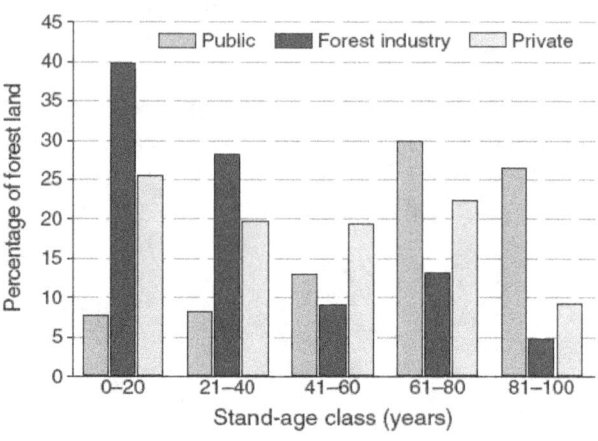

Figure 8—Percentage of forest land area by ownership class and stand-age class, Virginia, 2007.

The Virginia State champion sassafras, which measures just under 72 inches d.b.h., is in Lee county, VA. (photo by Harold Jerrell, Lee County, VA, Virginia Cooperative Extension)

Stand-Level Volume and Number of Trees

Volume of live trees ≥ 5.0 inches d.b.h. on all forest land increased from 31.5 billion cubic feet in 2001 to 32.8 billion cubic feet in 2007, an increase of 4 percent. Change in volume was not uniform across the State. Total volume in the Coastal Plain decreased by 126.8 million cubic feet, or 1.6 percent, while the volume per acre there increased by 1.5 percent. Volume in the Northern Piedmont increased by 547.5 million cubic feet, or 10 percent. The Northern Piedmont continued to have the highest volume per acre, at 2,335.6 cubic feet per acre, and the Southern Piedmont had the least, at 1,902.5 cubic feet per acre (table 2).

Volume of live trees on forest industry land increased by 13 percent, from 1,400.9 cubic feet per acre in 2001 to 1,584.4 cubic feet per acre in 2007 (table 2). Volume on public land went from 2,197.7 to 2,317.6 cubic feet per acre, and volume on NIPF land went from 1,994.6 to 2,056.8 cubic feet per acre. The number of live trees ≥ 1.0 inch d.b.h. remained steady at 11.2 billion stems, 77 percent of which were 1.0 to 4.9 inches d.b.h. Increases were noted in all size classes, except those in the 3.0- to 8.9-inch range.

Table 2—Volume of live trees per acre on forest land by survey year, unit, and ownership class, Virginia

Survey year and unit	All classes	Ownership class		
		Public	Forest industry	Nonindustrial private
		cubic feet per acre		
2001				
Coastal Plain	2,076.5	3,371.4	1,408.2	2,044.3
Southern Piedmont	1,758.0	2,262.4	1,186.3	1,777.8
Northern Piedmont	2,202.9	2,202.0	1,440.8	2,246.5
Northern Mountains	1,882.9	1,866.1	1,543.5	1,916.0
Southern Mountains	2,102.2	2,313.2	1,788.0	2,067.6
All units	1,991.1	2,197.7	1,400.9	1,994.7
2007				
Coastal Plain	2,107.7	3,258.2	1,440.2	2,042.6
Southern Piedmont	1,902.5	2,296.7	1,954.0	1,875.8
Northern Piedmont	2,335.6	2,304.8	1,089.1	2,374.7
Northern Mountains	2,020.7	2,031.0	2,049.1	2,010.4
Southern Mountains	2,141.1	2,453.1	1,568.9	2,077.1
All units	2,086.6	2,317.6	1,584.4	2,056.8

Softwoods

Live softwood volume on forest land increased from 7.1 billion cubic feet in 2001 to 7.5 billion cubic feet in 2007. By unit, live-tree softwood volume decreased by 6 percent in the Southern Mountains and increased by 17 percent in the Northern Mountains. Increases in volume were noted in most diameter classes, with the exception of trees 5.0 to 6.9 and 19.0 to 20.9 inches d.b.h. (fig. 9). Volume increased by 11 and 15 percent in trees 11.0 to 12.9 and 15.0 to 16.9 inches d.b.h., respectively. Sixty-seven percent of softwood volume was in trees < 13.0 inches d.b.h. The number of live softwood trees ≥ 1.0 inch d.b.h. increased by 4 percent, from 2.0 to 2.1 billion stems.

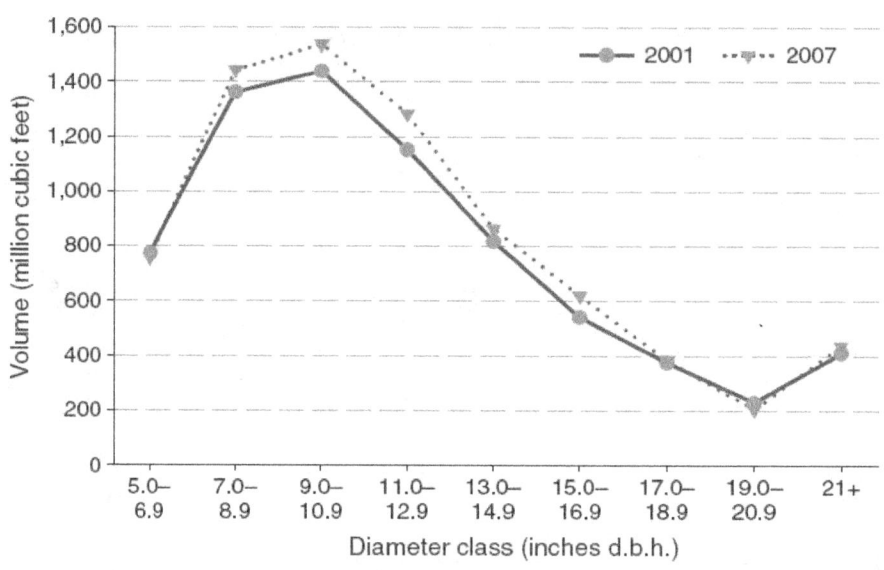

Figure 9—Volume of live softwoods on forest land by diameter class, Virginia, 2001 and 2007.

Dogwood, the Virginia State tree. (photo by Harold Jerrell, Lee County, VA, Virginia Cooperative Extension)

Hardwoods

Hardwood live-tree volume on forest land continued to increase, from 24.4 billion cubic feet in 2001 to 25.3 billion cubic feet in 2007, a 3-percent change. The largest increase occurred in the Northern Piedmont, where live-tree volume rose by 456.7 million cubic feet, a 10-percent change. In contrast, there was a decrease in hardwood volume in the Coastal Plain of 115.8 million cubic feet, a 2-percent change.

Hardwood volume decreased in the four smallest diameter classes (fig. 10). The largest percentage change was the 15-percent increase in volume of trees over 20.9 inches d.b.h. While 67 percent of softwood volume was in trees < 13.0 inches d.b.h., only 40 percent of hardwood volume was in trees of that size. The number of live hardwoods ≥ 1.0 inch d.b.h. decreased by 1 percent, from 9.1 to 9.0 billion stems.

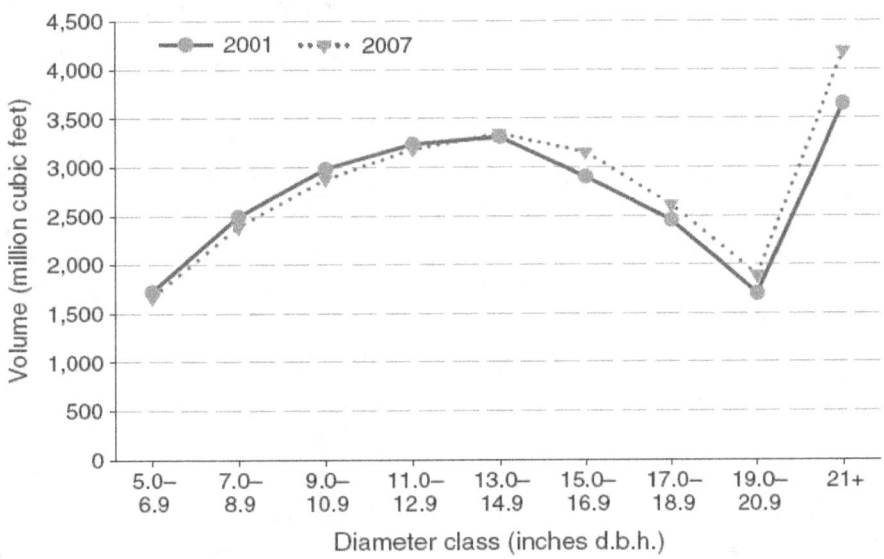

Figure 10—Volume of live hardwoods on forest land by diameter class, Virginia, 2001 and 2007.

Yellow-poplar and red maple line a country road in the Silver Leaf Community, Lee County, VA. (photo by Harold Jerrell, Lee County, VA, Virginia Cooperative Extension)

Species Importance

Volume

Yellow-poplar continued to rank first for live-tree volume with 5.0 billion cubic feet in 2007, an increase of 9 percent from 2001 (table 3). This species contained 15 percent of the live-tree volume for all trees ≥ 5.0 inches d.b.h. Since 1992, this species increased by 38 percent (fig. 11). Loblolly pine was the second most dominant species and increased by 13 percent, to 4.2 billion cubic feet. It was the predominant softwood species, accounting for 56 percent of the softwood live-tree volume. Loblolly pine showed the largest gain in volume of any single species in Virginia, increasing by 465.8 million cubic feet. Since 1992, this species increased by 39 percent on timberland (fig. 11). Chestnut oak, white oak, and red maple continued to rank next in live-tree volume. Altogether, the top five species made up 17.5 billion cubic feet, or 53 percent of the State's live-tree volume on forest land. Virginia pine and eastern white pine were still the second and third ranked softwoods for volume.

Chestnut oak.
(photo by Anita K. Rose)

Table 3—Top 50 tree species dominant for volume (≥ 5.0 inches d.b.h.) on forest land, Virginia, 2007

Species	Volume
	million cubic feet
Yellow-poplar	5,018.2
Loblolly pine	4,189.5
Chestnut oak	3,055.9
White oak	2,988.3
Red maple	2,253.8
Northern red oak	1,638.9
Virginia pine	1,470.4
Sweetgum	1,115.0
Scarlet oak	1,028.1
Black oak	1,018.4
Eastern white pine	777.9
Pignut hickory	663.4
Mockernut hickory	613.6
Southern red oak	573.9
American beech	570.4
Blackgum	387.4
Sugar maple	383.6
White ash	376.2
Shortleaf pine	304.9
Sweet birch	283.4
American sycamore	252.6
Black cherry	236.3
Black locust	235.4
Pitch pine	205.8
American basswood	199.5
Eastern hemlock	189.1
Green ash	187.8
Eastern redcedar	187.2
Sourwood	182.1
Swamp tupelo	168.7
Willow oak	153.2
Black walnut	133.3
Bitternut hickory	131.2
Cucumbertree	127.1
Shagbark hickory	119.1
River birch	94.3
Post oak	92.8
Table Mountain pine	84.8
Sassafras	73.0
American holly	71.4
Swamp chestnut oak	69.4
Ailanthus	67.3
American elm	60.9
Yellow buckeye	57.0
Baldcypress	54.4
Slippery elm	47.7
Cherrybark oak	46.2
Red spruce	45.3
Water tupelo	44.1
Chinkapin oak	41.5

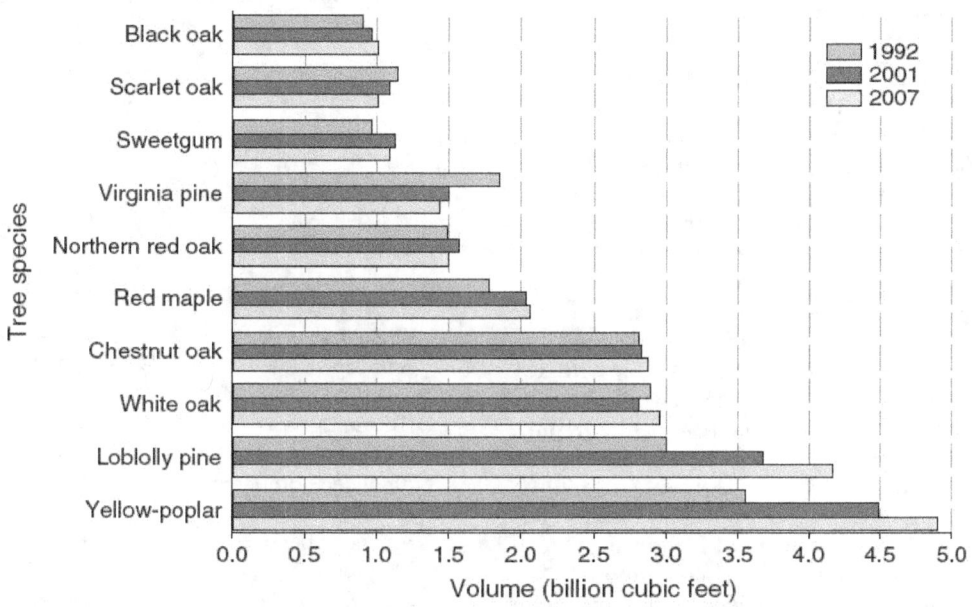

Figure 11—Live volume on timberland for the top 10 species (2007 volume) by survey year, Virginia.

Species dominance varied by unit. Yellow-poplar ranked first for volume in both Piedmont units and the Southern Mountains, and ranked second on the Coastal Plain. It accounted for between 7 and 22 percent of the volume in each of the five units. Loblolly pine was first for volume on the Coastal Plain and was second on the Southern Piedmont, accounting for 34 and 17 percent of the volume in those units, respectively. Volume in the Northern Mountains was dominated by chestnut oak, which accounted for 1.4 billion cubic feet, or 25 percent of the live-tree volume.

At the genus level, oaks dominated the volume of live trees (10.8 billion cubic feet) and pines were second (7.0 billion cubic feet). For number of trees, pines ranked first (701.8 million) and oaks second (619.7 million). Together, oaks and pines accounted for 54 percent of the volume and 52 percent of the live trees ≥ 5.0 inches d.b.h.

Species dominance or importance can be affected by artificial regeneration. A species such as loblolly pine, which tends to be the species of choice in softwood plantations, can have a much higher ranking than would naturally be expected due to the influence of plantings. This species had the highest percentage of its volume in planted stands (65 percent).

Number of Trees

Typically, the species that dominate volume also tend to dominate the number of trees. However, some very common species can be numerous, and may be considered dominant where this is the case, but because of their growth form are not dominant in terms of volume.

Although there was a 3.5-percent decrease, red maple continued to rank first, for number of trees ≥ 1.0 inch d.b.h., with 1.4 billion stems; this represented 13 percent of the total number (table 4). Loblolly pine was second, with just over 1.0 billion live stems, an increase of 9 percent since 2001. Yellow-poplar, sweetgum, and blackgum were third, fourth, and fifth for number of stems. Yellow-poplar accounted for 8 percent, and both sweetgum and blackgum accounted for 6 percent of all live stems. These top five species represented 41 percent of all live stems.

Flowering dogwood and American holly were both in the top 10 for number of trees. This illustrates how a species of relatively small stature can play an important role in a forest ecosystem.

Red maple was dominant for number of live stems in both Piedmont units and the Southern Mountains, where it accounted for 12 to 15 percent of live stems. Blackgum was dominant in the Northern Mountains, where it accounted for 15 percent of the live stems. Loblolly pine was dominant in the Coastal Plain, where it accounted for 20 percent of the live stems.

Table 4—Top 50 tree species dominant for number of stems (≥ 1.0 inch d.b.h.) on forest land, Virginia, 2007

Species	Number
	thousand trees
Red maple	1,423,077.7
Loblolly pine	1,041,614.7
Yellow-poplar	846,500.3
Sweetgum	682,096.9
Blackgum	619,730.2
Virginia pine	490,996.6
White oak	438,343.4
American holly	424,257.8
Chestnut oak	361,631.9
Flowering dogwood	331,891.4
Sourwood	323,844.6
American hornbeam	288,112.7
Eastern redcedar	249,221.9
American beech	214,804.9
Black cherry	205,448.4
Mockernut hickory	197,760.6
Pignut hickory	185,395.8
Eastern white pine	171,091.7
Sugar maple	163,945.5
Scarlet oak	160,794.1
Sassafras	157,302.9
Southern red oak	151,764.9
Northern red oak	147,742.6
Eastern redbud	139,378.1
Black oak	127,755.1
Black locust	113,765.7
Sweet birch	109,177.2
White ash	106,792.7
Striped maple	92,341.7
Serviceberry spp.	76,064.8
Ailanthus	70,751.6
Green ash	69,517.6
Willow oak	60,046.3
Winged elm	55,641.3
Shortleaf pine	55,285.0
Water oak	50,677.9
Eastern hemlock	48,194.4
American elm	47,870.8
River birch	41,144.3
Eastern hophornbeam	34,016.8
Post oak	33,750.5
Swamp tupelo	31,097.8
Fraser magnolia	28,337.2
Sweetbay	28,044.3
Pawpaw	27,161.6
Pitch pine	24,668.3
American basswood	23,552.5
American sycamore	21,475.8
Hawthorn spp.	20,538.4
Slippery elm	19,173.4

The Status of Oak Regeneration

There is some evidence that oak-dominated forests of the Eastern United States may be transitioning to more maple- and mixed-species-dominated forests. Although oaks are still major overstory dominants, they are often underrepresented in the understory (Abrams and Copenheaver 1999, Cole and Ware 1997, Farrell and Ware 1991). This lack of understory dominance is often attributed to the low-shade tolerance of oaks and to the lack of disturbance, primarily from fire suppression (Abrams 1992, Burns and Honkala 1990). Whether shade-tolerant, fire-sensitive species, such as red maple, will assume a dominant overstory position in the future is uncertain. In relatively undisturbed stands across Virginia, it appears that most oak species occur on far fewer plots in the sapling-size class than the tree-size class (Rose 2008). Results from the current survey showed that, on a per-acre basis, red maple was by far the most dominant sapling-size tree (fig. 12). At the survey-unit level, this was also true in both Piedmont units and the Southern Mountains (table 5). White oak regeneration was most prevalent in the Southern and Northern Piedmont, while chestnut oak saplings were most numerous in the Northern Mountains.

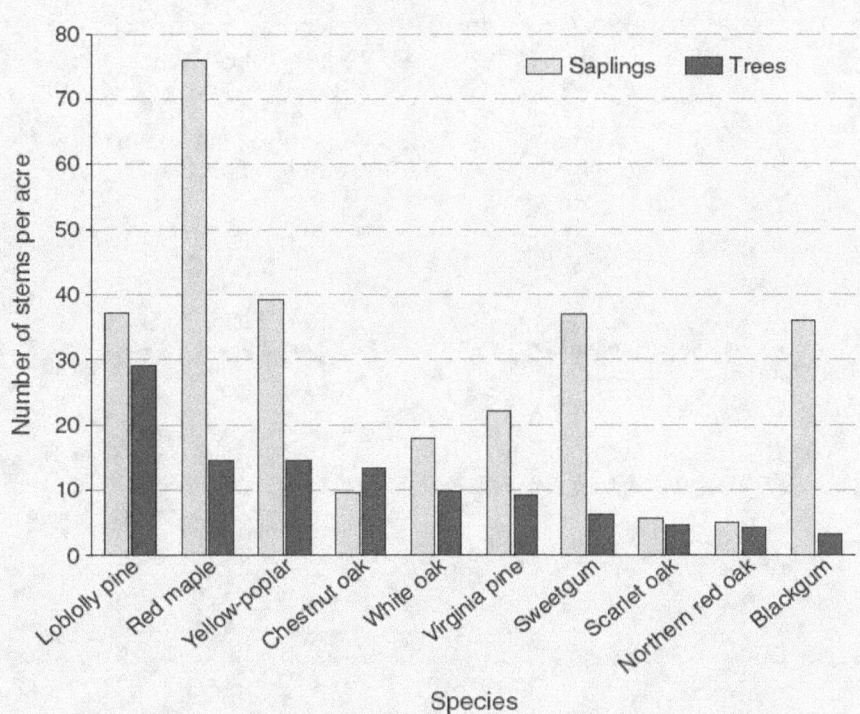

Figure 12—Number of saplings (1.0 to 4.9 inches d.b.h.) and trees (≥ 5.0 inches d.b.h.) per acre by species, Virginia, 2007.

Chestnut oak.
(photo by Anita K. Rose)

Across Virginia, the regeneration potential of oak species appears low compared to other species. The canopy tree species with the highest sapling densities tended to be the mesic, shade-tolerant ones, in particular red maple and blackgum. It is possible that without disturbance these species will increase in abundance and oak species will decrease.

Table 5—Number of saplings (1.0 to 4.9 inches d.b.h.) and trees (≥ 5.0 inches d.b.h.) per acre on forest land by species and survey unit, Virginia, 2007

Species	All units		Coastal Plain		Southern Piedmont		Northern Piedmont		Northern Mountains		Southern Mountains	
	Saplings	Trees	Saplings	Trees	Saplings	Trees	Saplings	Trees	Saplings	Trees	Saplings	Trees
					stems per acre							
American beech	11.2	2.5	13.8	3.6	11.8	2.1	12.2	2.9	1.9	0.2	14.6	3.2
Black locust	5.4	1.9	3.4	0.3	3.2	0.8	3.8	1.4	7.7	2.3	9.6	5.2
Black oak	4.8	3.3	5.6	2.0	5.7	1.8	4.9	3.3	3.3	6.1	4.0	4.5
Blackgum	36.1	3.3	17.2	2.5	35.4	2.9	32.6	3.0	76.2	5.9	27.2	2.7
Chestnut oak	9.6	13.4	1.2	0.9	14.5	7.0	6.2	9.0	18.7	37.8	8.6	18.2
Eastern hemlock	1.9	1.1	—	—	—	0.1	1.9	0.3	2.4	2.6	6.1	3.2
Eastern redcedar	13.5	2.3	6.8	0.5	23.5	2.5	25.2	5.2	7.2	2.3	5.4	2.1
Eastern white pine	7.2	3.6	—	0.0	3.3	0.7	1.8	1.9	21.0	9.0	13.1	8.3
Green ash	3.4	1.0	4.9	1.6	5.8	1.3	3.0	0.6	1.0	0.7	1.3	0.4
Loblolly pine	37.3	29.0	106.0	68.8	42.0	43.2	13.8	14.9	0.7	0.8	—	0.1
Mockernut hickory	9.5	3.1	7.1	1.6	17.0	3.6	8.3	4.4	9.6	2.9	4.2	3.1
Northern red oak	5.1	4.3	1.5	0.9	7.3	2.8	2.8	4.8	6.5	8.3	7.4	6.4
Pignut hickory	8.6	3.2	5.6	1.3	9.7	2.0	13.9	5.6	10.3	4.6	5.2	3.6
Red maple	75.9	14.6	84.0	13.8	94.9	13.6	62.1	12.8	62.4	13.2	66.2	19.5
Scarlet oak	5.7	4.5	7.5	1.9	5.1	2.4	4.1	3.2	5.2	9.9	6.1	6.6
Sourwood	17.7	2.9	15.7	0.8	34.9	5.3	1.4	0.5	4.1	0.7	24.4	6.3
Southern red oak	7.7	2.0	14.2	3.1	11.9	2.6	9.4	3.9	—	0.1	—	0.0
Sugar maple	8.5	1.9	0.2	—	1.4	0.1	2.3	0.3	11.3	3.0	29.7	6.8
Sweetgum	37.1	6.2	95.8	16.2	54.4	7.6	10.3	3.9	—	—	—	0.1
Virginia pine	22.1	9.1	11.9	4.7	57.1	17.8	20.9	13.6	9.7	7.1	3.6	2.2
White ash	5.0	1.8	1.0	0.7	5.4	0.8	10.2	3.2	5.0	1.8	5.0	3.3
White oak	18.0	9.9	15.8	8.9	29.7	10.8	27.9	12.8	8.4	11.7	6.8	5.8
Yellow-poplar	39.2	14.6	48.5	12.8	67.1	19.3	32.8	17.7	10.5	5.5	24.6	16.4

— = no sample for the cell; 0.0 = a value of > 0.0 but < 0.05 for the cell.

Growth, Removals, and Mortality

Three major components of change were monitored in the Virginia survey: growth, removals, and mortality. Complex interactions among these components can result in increases or decreases in the inventory. Estimates are given as an annual average and reflect the status of trees measured in the 2001 survey and then remeasured in the 2007 survey. Gross growth minus mortality equals net growth, and net growth minus removals equals either a positive or negative net change in volume for the total forest resource.

Net growth for all live trees on timberland averaged 1,030.4 million cubic feet per year (table 6). This was an increase of 4.1 percent from the 2001 survey, when it

Jamestown Island Colonial National Historic Park. (photo by Anita K. Rose)

Table 6—Average net annual growth, removals, and mortality of all live trees on timberland by species group and survey unit, Virginia, 2002 to 2007

Component and species group	All units	Coastal Plain	Southern Piedmont	Northern Piedmont	Northern Mountains	Southern Mountains
				million cubic feet		
Growth						
Softwoods	398.9	187.7	136.0	46.4	17.1	11.8
Hardwoods	631.5	119.3	167.7	119.9	69.8	154.8
All species	1,030.4	306.9	303.7	166.3	86.9	166.6
Removals						
Softwoods	340.6	189.8	97.2	35.1	6.1	12.4
Hardwoods	487.0	146.1	99.5	93.1	59.3	88.9
All species	827.5	335.9	196.7	128.2	65.3	101.4
Mortality						
Softwoods	96.6	37.4	23.3	9.9	9.7	16.4
Hardwoods	189.3	54.9	31.1	36.4	34.1	32.8
All species	286.0	92.3	54.4	46.3	43.8	49.1

Numbers in rows and columns may not sum to totals due to rounding.

averaged 990.0 million cubic feet per year. Net growth of hardwoods decreased from 662.9 to 631.5 million cubic feet per year, while net growth of softwoods increased from 327.2 to 398.9 million cubic feet per year. Loblolly pine accounted for 31 percent of net growth for all live trees, and 80 percent of growth for softwoods. Softwood net growth increased in all units, except the Southern Mountains, where it declined from 14.4 to 11.8 million cubic feet per year. Hardwood net growth increased in both Piedmont units and the Southern Mountains, but decreased in the Coastal Plain and the Northern Mountains. The change was most dramatic in the Coastal Plain, where hardwood net growth fell by 20 percent, from 149.8 to 119.3 million cubic feet per year.

Evaluation of growth on a per-acre basis minimizes the effects of shifts in ownership that took place in Virginia since the 2001 survey. Net growth of all live trees averaged 67.6 cubic feet per acre per year across the State. This was an increase of 6 percent. At 92.4 cubic feet per acre per year, net growth was highest on forest-industry owned land (fig. 13). This was an increase of 3.1 cubic feet per acre per year. The high growth rate on forest industry land is a reflection of the large proportion of plantations in the most productive age classes on that land. There was a 7-percent increase in net growth on NIPF land, from 67.7 to 72.1 cubic feet per acre per year. In addition, net growth on public land increased from 34.0 to 38.0 cubic feet per acre per year. The relatively low amount of growth on public land is a reflection of the large proportion of land in the sawtimber stand-size class.

Live-tree removals on timberland averaged 827.5 million cubic feet per year (table 6). This was an increase of 19 percent from the 2001 survey, when removals averaged 697.9 million cubic feet per year. Nearly 70 percent of this increase was in hardwood removals. Although 23 percent of inventory volume was in softwoods and 77 percent

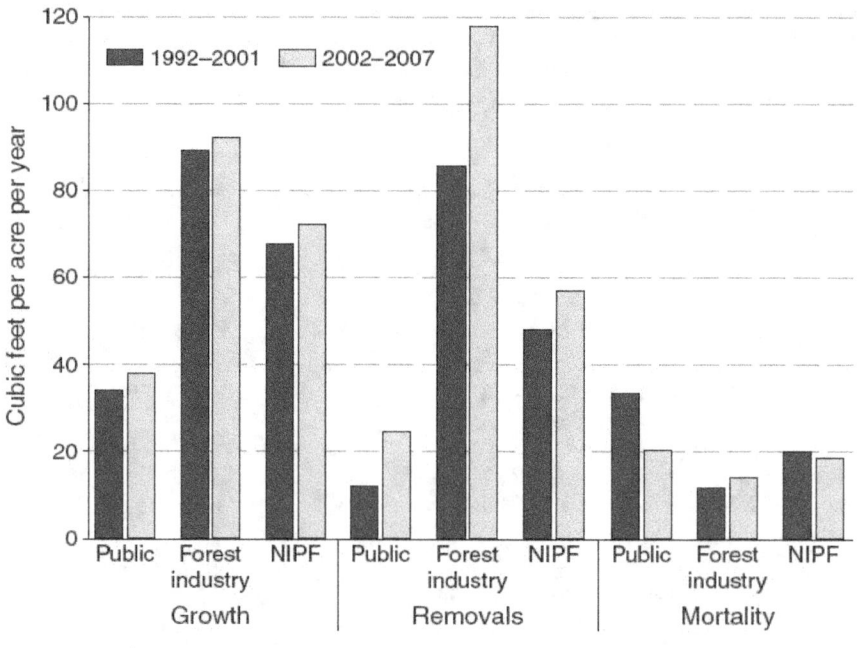

Figure 13—Average net annual growth, removals, and mortality per acre on timberland by ownership class and survey period, Virginia (NIPF = nonindustrial private forest).

in hardwoods, 41 percent of the volume of live-tree removals consisted of softwoods and 59 percent of hardwoods. Removals increased in all units except the Southern Piedmont. In the Coastal Plain removals were up substantially, from 247.4 to 335.9 million cubic feet, a 36-percent increase. Removals also increased substantially in the Northern Piedmont and Northern Mountains. The increases in removals may be associated with Hurricane Isabel, which moved through the State in September 2003 (see Disturbance section).

Overall, the ratio of live net growth to live removals was 1.2:1.0. This indicates that net growth exceeded harvesting in Virginia. The softwood growth-to-removals ratio was 1.2:1.0, and the hardwood growth-to-removals ratio was 1.3:1.0. When ratios approach 1.0:1.0, there is a high likelihood that removals exceeded growth in several areas in the State. Ideally, if harvesting is to be sustainable, removals should not exceed growth for long periods. Although softwood removals did exceed growth in the Southern Mountains, growth of softwoods and hardwoods combined exceeded removals in all units except the Coastal Plain, the area most affected by Hurricane Isabel. Loblolly pine accounted for 28 percent of all removals.

On a per-acre basis, removals of live trees increased from 45.1 to 54.3 cubic feet per acre per year. Rates of removals, like rates of growth, were highest on forest-industry owned land, where the most significant increase in removals also occurred. Here, rates of removals increased by 32.3 cubic feet per acre per year to 117.9 cubic feet

per acre per year (38 percent) (fig. 13). The increase in removals per acre was more than the increase in growth per acre on industry lands, and resulted in removals exceeding growth. Removals increased by 12.2 cubic feet per acre per year (100 percent) on public lands, and increased by 9.0 cubic feet per acre per year (19 percent) on NIPF land.

Across the State, mortality averaged 286.0 million cubic feet per year (table 6). This was a 14-percent decrease since the 2001 survey, when mortality averaged 333.6 million cubic feet per year. Mortality decreased in all units, except for the Coastal Plain, where there was a 47-percent increase, from 62.8 to 92.3 million cubic feet per year. Per-acre mortality decreased on public land, from 33.5 to 20.5 cubic feet per acre per year (by 39 percent) (fig. 13). On forest industry land, per-acre mortality increased by 20 percent, and on NIPF land it decreased by 7 percent.

Basswood, Russell County, VA.
(photo by Anita K. Rose)

19

Disturbance

Management activities, especially the establishment of plantations, can impact stand structure by altering forest type, species composition, stand age, stand density, and other stand attributes. In 2007, 2.4 million acres of timberland in Virginia were classified as planted, and 12.9 million acres were classified as natural. Eighty-four percent (2.0 million acres) of all planted stands were in the Coastal Plain and Southern Piedmont. Between the 2001 survey and the 2007 survey, timberland area classified as planted increased by 12 percent (251,200 acres), and between the 1992 survey and the 2001 survey it increased by 21 percent (364,400 acres). From 1986 to 2007, the area of planted stands increased by almost 1.0 million acres, from 1.4 to 2.4 million acres, a 69-percent change. Nearly all of the planted acreage was in the loblolly-shortleaf forest-type group. The oak-pine and oak-hickory forest-type groups occupied most of the remaining area classified as planted.

The rate of plantings increased slightly, from 62,100 acres per year in the 2001 survey to 74,700 acres per year in the 2007 survey. However, not all of this resulted from conversion of natural to planted stands. Just over 25 percent of the artificial regeneration that occurred between surveys took place on stands that had been established by plantings sometime before the 2001 survey. Also, a small portion of the new plantings were afforestation efforts on land denoted as nonforest in the previous survey.

The rate of clearcutting decreased by 9 percent, from 146,900 acres per year in the 2001 survey to 133,600 acres per year in the 2007 survey. In contrast, partial harvesting increased by 7 percent, from 110,600 to 117,900 acres per year.

Weather-caused disturbance, including events such as wind, ice, flooding, hurricanes, or tornadoes, affected an estimated 3 percent of Virginia's forest land since 2001. The amount of acreage impacted by weather decreased in all units, except the Coastal Plain, where it increased by 54 percent. Nearly one-half of all weather-related disturbance occurred in that area, and 217,700 acres were affected, probably a result of Hurricane Isabel.

Rain curtain from approaching storm, Madison County, VA. (photo by Anita K. Rose)

Hurricane Isabel

In September 2003 Hurricane Isabel made landfall on the Outer Banks of North Carolina. Identified as a category 2 hurricane, the storm caused widespread wind and flood damage across eight States—from North Carolina to New York. Isabel passed through Virginia with sustained wind speeds ranging from 32 to 60 knots and with gusts of up to 79 knots (Beven and Cobb 2004). Rainfall from the hurricane averaged 4 to 7 inches over large portions of east-central Virginia, and rainfall in the Shenandoah Valley of northern Virginia averaged 8 to 12 inches (Beven and Cobb 2004). A total of 77 counties and independent cities across Virginia were declared disaster zones and the estimated economic loss was $925 million, greater than any of the other States through which Isabel passed (U.S. Department of Commerce 2004). Most weather-related disturbance measured during the 2007 survey occurred in 2003 (fig. 14).

Hurricane Isabel may help explain why removals increased substantially for hardwoods in the Northern Piedmont and the Northern Mountains, and increased for both hardwoods and softwoods in the Coastal Plain. It may also be part of the

Chesapeake Bay, Grandview Nature Preserve, Hampton, VA. (photo by Anita K. Rose)

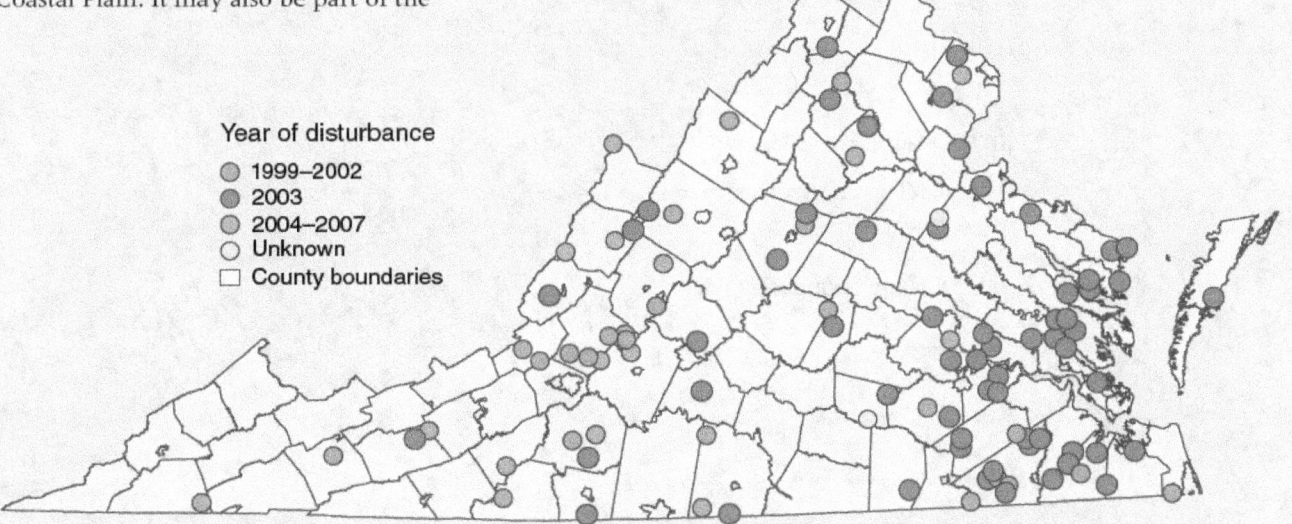

Year of disturbance
- 1999–2002
- 2003
- 2004–2007
- Unknown
- County boundaries

Figure 14—Plots affected by weather by year of disturbance, Virginia, 2007.

Rainbow, Madison County, VA. (photo by Anita K. Rose)

reason that mortality increased substantially for both hardwoods and softwoods in the Coastal Plain. Another potential impact of the hurricane was the significant increase in foliage transparency recorded after 2003 (Randolph and Rose 2009). Only 11 percent of P3 plots measured prior to the hurricane (2001 through 2003) had average transparencies of > 25 percent (fig. 15A). In contrast, 43 percent of plots measured after the hurricane (2004 through 2006) had average transparencies of > 25 percent (fig. 15B). This was especially true in the Coastal Plain, where 76 percent of plots measured after the hurricane had average foliage transparencies > 25 percent, while only 12 percent did prior to the hurricane.

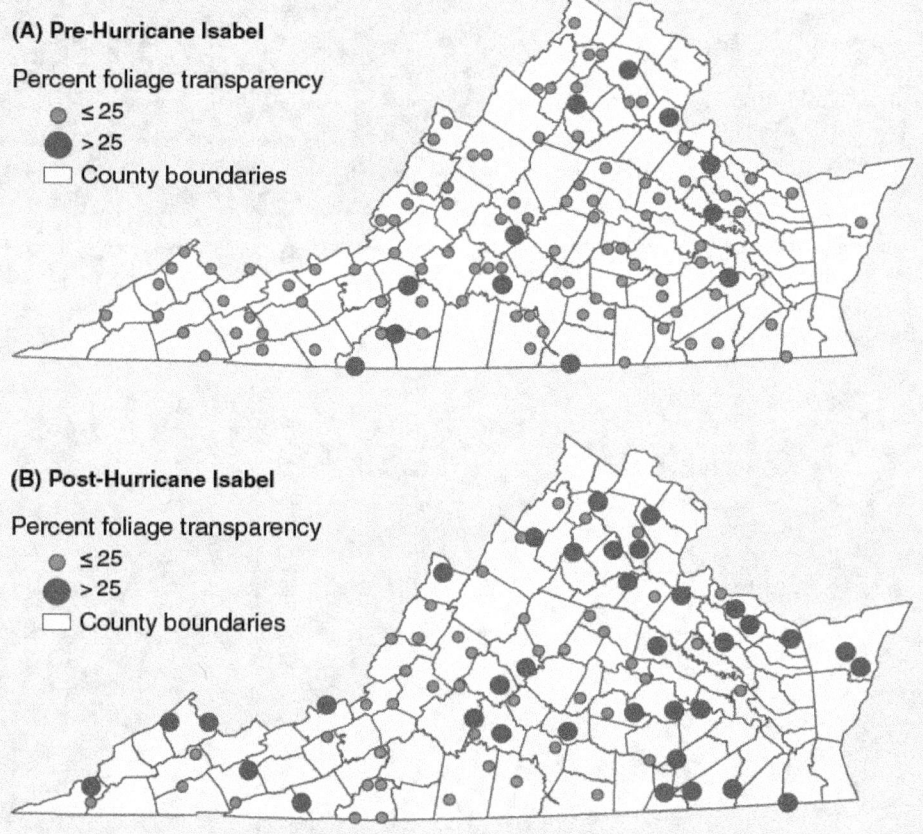

Figure 15—Foliage transparency on P3 plots, Virginia, (A) pre-Hurricane Isabel (2001–2003) and (B) post-Hurricane Isabel (2004–2006).

Insect Damage

Insect damage was the next most extensive natural disturbance, affecting 3 percent of Virginia's timberland. Over 50 percent of insect-related damage was in the Northern Mountains, where 8 percent of the timberland was affected. Much of the State's insect damage probably was caused by gypsy moth, southern pine beetle, and hemlock woolly adelgid.

Caterpillar, Botetourt County, VA. (photo by Anita K. Rose)

Pitch tubes indicating attacks of adult southern pine beetle on the trunk of a Virginia pine tree. (photo by Tim Tigner, Virginia Department of Forestry, www. forestryimages.org)

View from Graves Mountain, Shenandoah National Park in the distance, Madison County, VA. (photo by Anita K. Rose)

Invasive Exotic Species

Nonnative invasive plants pose a threat to the health of forests across the United States. Through competitive exclusion, suppression via allelopathy, and various other methods, invasive plants can suppress tree regeneration and reduce herbaceous species diversity (Merriam and Feil 2002, Orr and others 2005). There is some evidence that past land use and current levels of land development are factors that strongly influence invasion (Lundgren and others 2004). Japanese honeysuckle, nonnative roses, and tree-of-heaven were the most often occurring invasive species in Virginia's forests (table 7). The occurrence of these species was not equal across the State. Japanese honeysuckle occurred most frequently in the Northern and Southern Piedmont. There were 11 counties where Japanese honeysuckle was noted on 60 percent or more of forested subplots. Six of

these were in the Southern Piedmont in the adjacent counties of Pittsylvania, Halifax, Charlotte, and in Cumberland, Powhatan, and Amelia Counties. Tree-of-heaven (or Ailanthus), the most commonly occurring invasive tree, occurred predominately along the western edge of the Northern Piedmont. Six of the top eight counties for occurrence of tree-of-heaven extend in a line running north to south, from Rappahannock to Amherst Counties. In those six counties, tree-of-heaven was noted on between 13 and 23 percent of forested subplots. Between the 2001 survey and 2007 survey, the number of tree-of-heaven increased by 30 percent, from 54.3 to 70.8 million trees. In addition, the volume of this species increased by 52 percent, from 44.4 to 67.3 million cubic feet. Paulownia, another invasive tree species, also increased in number of trees (from 2.4 to 8.5 million stems) and volume (3.6 to 9.7 million cubic feet).

Table 7—Occurrence of invasive species by survey unit, Virginia, 2007[a]

		Survey unit				
Species	All units	Coastal Plain	Southern Piedmont	Northern Piedmont	Northern Mountains	Southern Mountains
		percentage of forested subplots				
Japanese honeysuckle	28.7	31.9	44.2	43.7	9.4	9.0
Nonnative roses	7.8	2.1	5.2	10.3	6.8	16.9
Tree-of-heaven	4.3	1.2	4.9	10.0	4.6	2.2
Tall fescue	3.9	1.9	5.0	4.0	3.3	5.5
Chinese/European privet	2.8	1.4	4.7	4.0	2.7	1.5
Nepalese browntop	2.3	1.1	1.3	3.2	1.9	4.4
Bush honeysuckle	2.0	0.1	5.0	0.9	1.8	1.5
Autumn olive	1.5	0.4	0.2	2.0	1.8	3.9
Japanese/glossy privet	0.8	0.7	0.6	1.2	1.3	0.2
Chinese lespedeza	0.8	0.7	1.1	—	0.1	1.7
Royal paulownia	0.5	0.6	0.4	1.2	0.2	0.3
Shrubby lespedeza	0.4	0.2	0.7	0.2	0.1	0.7
Winged burning bush	0.2	—	0.1	0.3	0.6	0.2
Silktree, mimosa	0.2	0.4	0.2	0.1	0.1	0.0

— = no sample for the cell; 0.0 = a value of >0.0 but <0.05 for the cell.

[a] May not represent the true occurrence of each species, as only the top four present on a subplot are recorded.

With the exception of Japanese honey-suckle, cover, for most of the invasive species, was < 1 percent on over 30 percent of the subplots they occupied. Typically, the number of forested subplots where a species was noted was not directly proportional to the number of forested plots measured. This is because many species often were recorded on only one subplot. For example, nonnative roses were recorded on only one subplot on about one-half of the plots on which that species was found. So, while nonnative roses were on 8 percent of all forested subplots, they were recorded on 16 percent of all forested plots. When compared with other States, Virginia was

second only to Kentucky for nonnative rose and tall fescue. Virginia ranked first for tree-of-heaven, and Tennessee ranked second.

In addition to invasive plants, there are a number of invasive insects and diseases that are or have the potential to affect Virginia's forests. The gypsy moth, which first moved through northern Virginia in 1984, has impacted millions of acres of the State's forests. Due to the prevalence of oaks and large tracts of forest, defoliation caused by gypsy moth has occurred primarily in the Northern Mountains. It is estimated that this insect defoliated 225,605 acres between 2002 and 2007 (U.S. Department of

Multiflora Rose, Botetourt County, VA. (photo by Anita K. Rose)

Agriculture Forest Service 2008). Although this is less than one-half the 834,380 acres defoliated between1997 and 2001, there is concern that the recent drought may result in a resurgence of the insect (Asaro 2007).

In 2008, the emerald ash borer, an insect native to Asia that kills ash trees, was detected in Fairfax County, Virginia. Ash trees are killed when larvae feed underneath the bark. There are about 177.6 million ash trees ≥ 1.0 inch d.b.h., and 566.0 million cubic feet of volume in

Emerald ash borer. (photo by David Cappaert, Michigan State University, www.Bugwood.org)

ash trees ≥ 5.0 inches d.b.h. White ash and green ash are the predominate species of ash in Virginia. The highest concentration of white ash was in the Northern Piedmont and the Mountains, while the highest concentration of green ash was in the Coastal Plain and Southern Piedmont (table 5). Efforts are under way to quarantine areas where the borer has been discovered in order to help prevent further spread of the insect. To find out more information, please visit the emerald ash borer Web site at http://www.emeraldashborer.info/.

Beech bark disease, the interaction of a scale insect and a fungus, has the potential to alter the character of forests in which beech is a constituent. Fortunately, some beech trees show a natural resistance and the rate of spread of this disease is fairly slow (Lovett and others 2006). Stem density of beech is highest in the Coastal Plain (3.6 trees per acre) followed by the Southern Mountains (3.2 trees per acre) (table 5).

Eastern and Carolina hemlock are susceptible to many pests and pathogens. Of particular concern is the hemlock woolly adelgid. Since its introduction into Virginia in the 1950s, this insect has spread to most counties where hemlock occurs. Feeding on the phloem of hemlock twigs, tree death typically occurs within 4 to 5 years (Lovett and others 2006). Symptoms of adelgid infestation include poor crown condition, conspicuous woollike ovisacs on underside of branch tips, and areas of extensive hemlock mortality and decline (U.S. Department of Agriculture Forest Service 2005). Hemlock is most prevalent in the Northern and Southern Mountains (table 5), where this insect is expected to cause a marked reduction in hemlock populations.

Hemlock woolly adelgid. (photo by Connecticut Agricultural Experiment Station Archive, Connecticut Agricultural Experiment Station, www.Bugwood.org)

Forest Health

FIA assesses several additional indicators to aid in the detection of potential forest health issues that may warrant further evaluation. These P3 indicators include ozone-induced injury, crown condition, down woody material, and soil condition. Readers should be aware that these indicators are based on a smaller plot population than the regular phase 2 (P2) sample, where approximately 1 out of every 16 P2 plots is a P3 plot, or 1 plot per 96,000 acres.

Ozone

Ozone is the product of chemical reactions that take place in the air when volatile organic compounds (VOC) mix and react with nitrogen oxides (NO_x) in the presence of sunlight. Anthropogenic emissions, primarily through the combustion of organic compounds, i.e., gasoline and coal, account for the most input of NO_x into the environment. In contrast, VOCs come primarily from natural sources, such as trees and other vegetation, although a sizable portion of the total input of VOCs does come from industrial and vehicular emissions. Weather plays a key role in the formation of ozone, with hot, dry, calm, cloudless days providing ideal conditions for VOCs and NO_x to combine and react to form ozone (U.S. Environmental Protection Agency 2004).

During the summer months, ozone concentrations at known phytotoxic levels can occur. A number of plants are sensitive to ozone exposures above normal background levels. These bioindicator species, such as yellow-poplar and

Yellow-poplar, the most dominant species for volume in Virginia. (photo by Harold Jerrell, Lee County, VA, Virginia Cooperative Extension)

sweetgum, exhibit an upper surface foliar injury symptom that can be distinguished from other foliar injuries. FIA tracks foliar injury to determine where negative impacts to forest trees may be occurring.

Ozone phytotoxicity is evaluated by field personnel statewide between late July and mid-August (U.S. Department of Agriculture Forest Service 2004b). The amount and severity of ozone injury varies according to a complex set of factors

Fern in the understory, Jamestown Island Colonial National Historic Park. (photo by Anita K. Rose)

including exposure, rates of stomatal uptake, and sensitivity to ozone. Studies have shown that periods of drought can offset the effects of ozone by reducing stomatal conductance (Patterson and others 2000). Variation in injury within a plant is largely determined by the position of the foliage, exposure to air and sunlight, and the age of the leaves.

During the 2007 survey, FIA evaluated 15,016 plants from various locations in Virginia (biosites), of which only 0.8 percent had ozone injury. This is in contrast to the previous survey (1997 to 2001), when 8 percent of plants had ozone injury. In the survey documented here, most of the injury occurred in 2003, while no injury was detected in 2005 (table 8). For each biosite, an index was calculated as the average score (amount x severity) for each species averaged across all species on the biosite. Only three biosites exhibited moderate-to-severe ozone injury (categories 3 and 4).

Excluding 2003, these field studies indicate that very little foliar injury due to ozone occurred across the State during the 2007 survey period. This was a change from the previous survey, when between 7 and 38 percent of biosites in every year, except for 1999, exhibited moderate-to-severe ozone injury. Hopefully, this trend of decreasing or very little ozone-induced injury will continue.

Table 8—Summary of ozone data for Virginia, 2007

Year	Plants		Biosites		Biosite index category			
	Evaluated	Injured	Evaluated	Injured	1	2	3	4
			number					
2002	1,820	1	24	1	23	1	—	—
2003	2,634	100	32	8	27	2	1	2
2004	3,822	11	39	5	39	—	—	—
2005	3,128	0	39	0	39	—	—	—
2006	3,612	9	38	2	38	—	—	—

— = no sample for the cell.

The Virginia State champion shagbark hickory, which is just over 43 inches d.b.h., is in Lee county, VA. (photo by Harold Jerrell, Lee County, VA, Virginia Cooperative Extension)

Crowns

Tree crowns are affected by many biotic and abiotic factors such as tree age, soil conditions, precipitation, air pollution, insects, and disease. Therefore, tree crown condition is a potential indicator of forest health. Monitoring for unusually poor crown conditions, or changes in crown conditions through time, can indicate areas of concern that may warrant further investigation. FIA measures several indicators to assess crown condition and to detect various states of crown decline. These include crown dieback, foliage transparency, crown density, and sapling crown vigor.

Crown dieback is recorded as percent mortality of the terminal portion of branches that are ≤ 1 inch in diameter, and are positioned in the upper portion of the crown (U.S. Department of Agriculture

Forest Service 2004b). High levels of dieback may indicate the presence of defoliating agents and a general loss of vigor. Increases in crown dieback indicate stress, possibly caused by root damage, stem damage that interferes with moisture and nutrient transport to the crown, or direct injury to the crown (Schomaker and others 2007). Crown dieback is considered an indication of recent stress because small dead twigs do not persist for long, and because trees typically replace lost twigs and foliage if the stress does not continue.

Average crown dieback across all plots was 3.3 percent. This was a slight increase from the previous survey, when dieback averaged 2.8 percent. By survey unit, average dieback ranged from a low of 2.0 percent in the Southern Piedmont to a high of 5.2 percent in the Northern Mountains. Most

hardwoods and softwoods had no crown dieback, 73 and 86 percent, respectively. Crown dieback varied by species, with black walnut, American elm, and willow oak having the highest percentage of trees with >15 percent dieback (table 9).

Foliage transparency is the percentage of skylight that is visible through the live, normally foliated part of the crown (Zarnoch and others 2004). High foliage transparency may be due to insect- or

Table 9—Crown density, crown dieback, and foliage transparency of trees (≥5.0 inches d.b.h.) by species group on P3 plots, Virginia, 2007

Species group	Trees	Crown density percent			Crown dieback percent			Foliage transparency percent		
		0–25	26–50	>50	0–5	6–15	>15	0–25	26–50	>50
	n	------------------ percentage of trees ------------------								
Softwoods										
Loblolly pine	883	10	76	14	96	3	1	56	43	2
Virginia pine	276	18	77	5	91	7	3	56	34	11
Eastern white pine	57	4	70	26	93	4	4	77	21	2
Eastern redcedar	36	6	42	53	94	6	0	81	17	3
Shortleaf pine	34	12	74	15	85	15	0	79	18	3
Pitch pine	15	0	93	7	87	13	0	60	40	0
Other softwoods	24	13	63	25	67	33	0	83	17	0
All softwoods	1,325	11	75	14	94	5	1	59	38	3
Hardwoods										
Chestnut oak	376	2	87	11	88	10	2	91	9	0
Yellow-poplar	314	3	74	24	94	3	3	81	19	0
Red maple	310	8	72	20	84	8	8	76	22	2
White oak	181	3	67	30	87	9	4	84	15	1
Sweetgum	145	6	72	23	89	8	3	74	23	3
Mockernut hickory	126	3	60	37	89	7	4	89	10	1
Black oak	93	1	82	17	81	17	2	84	16	0
Scarlet oak	88	1	93	6	66	26	8	83	17	0
Northern red oak	81	1	73	26	83	14	4	86	14	0
Sourwood	70	1	79	20	86	11	3	90	9	1
Pignut hickory	65	0	62	39	97	3	0	85	15	0
Blackgum	60	0	80	20	88	12	0	90	10	0
Sugar maple	56	2	57	41	75	14	11	82	16	2
Sweet birch	55	0	71	29	93	2	6	84	16	0
Black cherry	50	12	80	8	74	16	10	76	22	2
Southern red oak	50	10	68	22	86	8	6	58	42	0
American beech	45	7	44	49	87	11	2	80	20	0
Black locust	32	16	78	6	75	16	9	69	31	0
White ash	27	0	70	30	89	4	7	89	11	0
American basswood	20	0	35	65	85	15	0	100	0	0
Willow oak	18	11	67	22	89	0	11	61	28	11
Cucumbertree	17	0	47	53	100	0	0	100	0	0
American elm	16	0	88	13	75	13	13	81	19	0
Black walnut	15	0	73	27	73	13	13	67	33	0
Other hardwoods	175	7	68	25	87	8	5	82	15	3
All hardwoods	2,485	4	73	23	86	9	4	83	17	1

weather-related damage. Average foliage transparency for all plots was 25 percent. By unit, averages ranged from a low of 22 percent in the Northern Mountains to a high of 29 percent in the Coastal Plain. In contrast, foliage transparency averaged 17 percent in the Coastal Plain during the 2001 survey. This increase is probably due to Hurricane Isabel (Randolph and Rose, in press). Only 1 percent of hardwoods and 3 percent of softwoods had > 50 percent foliage transparency. Foliage transparency varied by species. Virginia pine and willow oak had the highest percentage of trees with > 50 percent transparency (table 9). For Virginia pine this is most likely an attribute of this species. The small sample size (n = 18) for willow oak probably resulted in an erroneously high percentage of trees in this category.

Crown density is the percentage of light blocked by branches, foliage, and reproductive structures relative to the total symmetrical crown outline (Zarnoch and others 2004). Average crown density on all plots was 44 percent, with survey unit averages ranging from 39 to 47 percent. Virginia pine, scarlet oak, and black locust had the lowest percentage of trees with > 50 percent crown densities (table 9).

Crown vigor class is used to rate the crown condition of saplings (trees 1.0 to 4.9 inches d.b.h.). Factors that can impact crown vigor in saplings include overhead competition and stand density. Separating natural stand competition functions from insect damage and disease damage is difficult. About 66 percent of all saplings were in vigor class 1 (good), 30 percent were in vigor class 2 (average), and only 4 percent were in vigor class 3 (poor). Sugar maple and flowering dogwood had the highest percentage of saplings in vigor class 3 (16 and 15 percent, respectively) (table 10). For dogwood, this may be indicative of dogwood anthracnose.

Table 10—Crown vigor ratings for saplings (1.0 to 4.9 inches d.b.h.) by species on P3 plots, Virginia, 2007

| Species | Saplings | Crown vigor | | |
| | | Good | Average | Poor |
	n	------ percentage ------		
Red maple	127	65	30	6
Yellow-poplar	86	71	27	2
Sweetgum	76	74	21	5
Loblolly pine	64	77	20	3
Blackgum	61	57	39	3
Shortleaf pine	42	93	7	0
Virginia pine	42	69	31	0
Sourwood	42	55	40	5
Eastern redcedar	40	63	38	0
Mockernut hickory	40	63	33	5
American hornbeam	37	46	54	0
Flowering dogwood	33	42	42	15
Black cherry	32	53	44	3
American holly	27	81	19	0
Pignut hickory	25	64	32	4
Southern red oak	25	76	24	0
White oak	23	83	9	9
American beech	21	81	14	5
Sugar maple	19	63	21	16
Chestnut oak	19	37	58	5
Eastern white pine	18	83	6	11
Eastern redbud	17	41	59	0
Willow oak	16	88	13	0
Striped maple	15	67	33	0
Other	197	66	30	4
Total	1,144	66	30	4

Big Cedar Creek near confluence with Clinch River, Pinnacle Natural Area Preserve, Russell County, VA. (photo by Anita K. Rose)

Evidence of wildlife activity on Jamestown Island Colonial National Historic Park. (photo by Anita K. Rose)

Soil

Soil is a key element of forest ecosystems. The characteristics of parent materials, from which soil is derived, partly determine what kind of plant life an ecosystem will support (Pritchett and Fisher 1987). Weathering is the primary means by which soils are formed. Over time, parent material is broken down into soil by precipitation, wind, and the freeze-thaw cycle. This is especially true in the Mountains and Piedmont units of Virginia. On the Coastal Plain, soils are considered relatively young geologically, having been formed by the deposition of continental sediments onto the submerged, shallow continental shelf, which was later exposed by sea level subsidence. Soil properties are also modified by soil organisms and the

decomposition of vegetation. Likewise, the modification of soils by natural means or human action can affect vegetation.

Erosion of soil is a primary concern due to the potential loss of nutrients from the upper layers of soil. Risk of significant erosion is greatest in areas with steep slopes, high precipitation, and large amounts of bare soil. The majority of P3 plots in Virginia (63 percent) had < 6 percent bare soil, while only 1 percent of plots had > 50 percent bare soil (fig. 16). The Northern Mountains had the fewest plots (39 percent) with 5 percent or less bare soil, and the Coastal Plain had the most (89 percent).

Soil compaction, most often a result of wheel traffic, reduces pore space and decreases air in the soil, thereby hindering root growth. The severity of compaction can vary by soil texture and percent moisture in the soil. Soils with multiple particle sizes, such as fine sandy loam, or high moisture content have a greater potential for damage (O'Neill and others 2005). On the majority of P3 plots (78 percent), < 6 percent of the plot area was compacted (fig. 16). More than 25 percent of the plot area was compacted on only 4 percent of plots. The

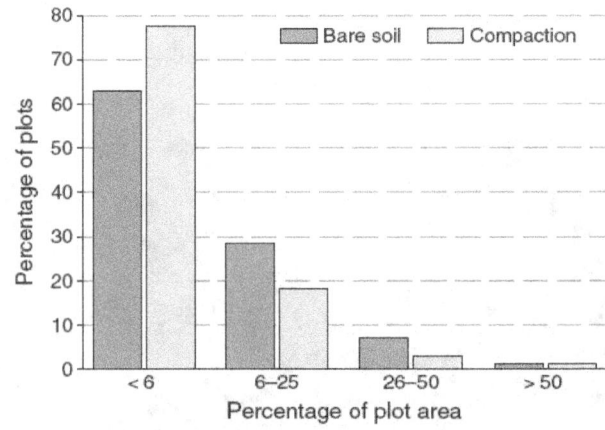

Figure 16—Distribution of bare soil and compaction on P3 plots, Virginia, 2007.

Southern Mountains had the fewest plots (67 percent) with < 6 percent compaction, and the Northern Piedmont had the most (89 percent).

The forest floor (duff and litter) averaged 1.9 inches thick. The Southern Piedmont had the lowest average, at 1.7 inches and the Northern Mountains had the highest, at 2.2 inches. Of neighboring Southern States, only North Carolina had a higher average than Virginia, with 2.2 inches of forest floor. In Virginia, the percentage of forest floor that was litter versus duff varied by unit. In the Coastal Plain and Southern Piedmont, duff was 34 percent of the forest floor, while in the Northern and Southern Mountains it was 42 and 43 percent, respectively.

Soil samples were also collected from P3 plots and analyzed in a laboratory for various physical and chemical properties to further clarify the status of forest soils. Mineral soil was collected in two layers, 0 to 4 inches (0–10 cm) (M1) and 4 to 8 inches (10–20 cm) (M2); and analyzed for percent carbon, nitrogen, pH, and a variety of exchangeable cations. Due to availability, this analysis includes soils collected in 2000 through 2004.

Bulk density, or the weight of a unit volume of dry soil, varies by soil texture. Clayey soils tend to have lower bulk densities than do sandy soils (Brady and Weil 1996). Forty-seven percent of the M1 samples were loamy, while 44 percent of the M2 samples were clayey. The threshold value for bulk density is typically considered 1.6 g/cm^3. At or above this threshold, root growth is impaired. Bulk density for the majority (59 percent) of M1 samples was < 1.20 g/cm^3. Sixty-two percent of M2 samples were > 1.39 g/cm^3 (fig. 17). Four percent of M1 and 30 percent of M2 samples had bulk densities ≥ 1.6 g/cm^3.

Soil pH, or the negative logarithm of the activity of hydrogen ions, affects all physical, chemical, and biological properties of a soil. It is a major factor determining what types of vegetation will dominate a natural landscape (Brady and Weil 1996). Most soils have a pH between 4.0 and 8.5 (Black 1957). The majority of the M1 and M2 samples had a pH < 5.1 (fig. 18). At these pH levels, enough exchangeable aluminum may be present to reduce plant growth.

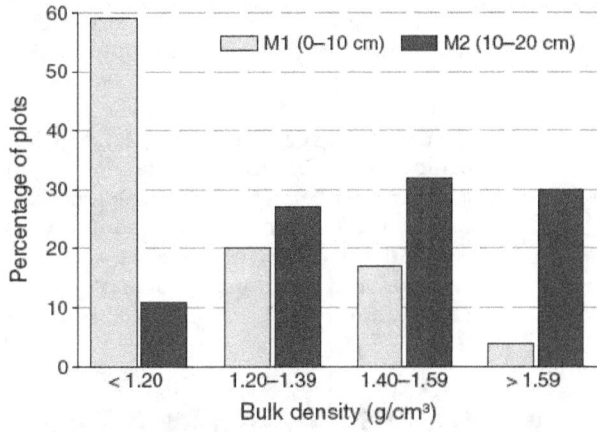

Figure 17—Distribution of bulk density values for mineral soils on P3 plots, Virginia, 2007.

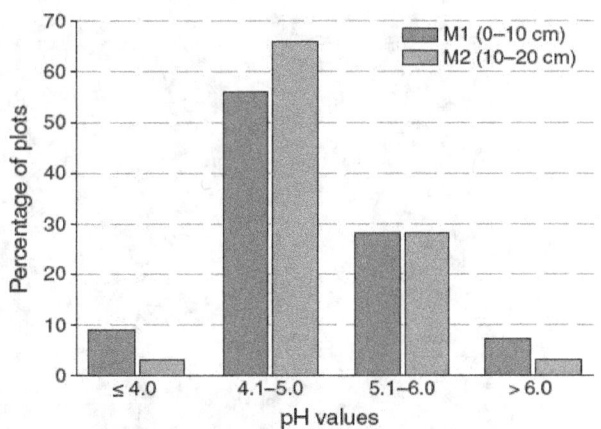

Figure 18—Distribution of pH values for mineral soils on P3 plots, Virginia, 2007.

Soil pH, base-forming cations such as calcium, and exchangeable aluminum are intricately related. As base-forming cations are leached from the soil, aluminum and hydrogen replace these much needed nutrients on the soil complex and pH decreases. Exchangeable aluminum averaged 127.6 and 136.1 mg/kg for the M1 and M2 layers, respectively. Exchangeable calcium averaged 471.5 mg/kg for the M1 layer and 178.5 mg/kg for the M2 layer.

In terrestrial systems, the amount of carbon in the soil often exceeds the amount found in the aboveground biomass. The organic carbon in soil includes decomposing material from plants and animals (Post and Kwon 2000, Schlesinger 1991). The M1 and M2 layers averaged 3.0 and 1.1 percent organic carbon, respectively. The mass of organic carbon per acre was calculated using the percent carbon of the sample and the bulk density. Together, the M1 and M2 layers averaged 16.8 tons per acre of organic carbon.

The status of soil on P3 plots in Virginia varied by unit and by the parameter considered. While soil erosion and compaction levels seemed low at the time, high bulk densities may be cause for concern. Likewise, low soil pH and high exchangeable aluminum are potential issues. Losses of base cations, such as calcium, from soils and the immobilization of soil aluminum may contribute to nutritional imbalances and ultimately to forest decline (Agren and Bosatta 1988, Garten and Van Miegroet 1994).

Deadwood

An important dynamic of any ecosystem is the return of nutrients to the system through decomposition. In forested ecosystems, deadwood can be a significant store of nutrients (Harmon and others 1987, Keenan and others 1993). Standing and down-dead trees are also important habitats for a wide variety of organisms, including invertebrates, small mammals, birds, reptiles, and amphibians. While many

Eastern painted turtle, Jamestown Island Colonial National Historic Park. (photo by Anita K. Rose)

Red tail hawk. (photo by Harold Jerrell, Lee County, VA, Virginia Cooperative Extension)

organisms depend on it, the presence of large amounts of deadwood can constitute a fire hazard.

Coarse woody debris (CWD) (down-dead logs ≥ 3.0 inches in diameter and ≥ 3.0 feet long) is particularly important as habitat and shelter for wildlife. Volume of CWD ranged from an average of 273.7 cubic feet per acre in the Coastal Plain to an average of 426.1 cubic feet per acre in the Southern Mountains. The average for the State was 326.5 cubic feet per acre (table 11).

Statewide, the density of CWD averaged 133 logs per acre. The density of CWD was lowest in the Southern Piedmont and highest in the Northern Mountains. Thirty-nine percent of plots had < 75 pieces of CWD per acre, and 15 percent of plots had zero pieces per acre. Deadwood goes through a number of physical, biological, and chemical changes during the decay process. Decomposition leads to the release of carbon dioxide, water, and nutrients, and to the production of stable organic

Table 11—Coarse woody debris attributes on P3 plots by survey unit, Virginia, 2007

Survey unit	Plots	CWD	Decay class					Size class[a]			
			1	2	3	4	5	3.0–7.9	8.0–12.9	13.0–17.9	≥ 18.0
	n	*ft³/acre*	------------------- pieces per acre -------------------								
Coastal Plain	38	273.7	12	22	43	36	8	109	10	0	0
Southern Piedmont	41	306.9	5	15	58	31	8	103	11	2	1
Northern Piedmont	27	304.4	1	34	62	38	8	133	9	1	0
Northern Mountains	28	351.9	8	30	83	25	6	142	9	1	1
Southern Mountains	27	426.1	2	13	84	30	19	131	15	1	2
Total	161	326.5	6	22	64	32	10	121	11	1	1

CWD = coarse woody debris.
[a] Diameter at transect (inches).

compounds known as humus (Schlesinger 1991). Boles begin to collapse, lose mass, and settle to the ground as they become unable to support their own weight. The majority of CWD was in decay classes 3 and 4 (table 11). Most of the CWD was 3.0 to 7.9 inches in diameter.

Biomass of CWD averaged 2.9 tons per acre statewide (table 12). The Northern Mountains had the most CWD per acre (3.5 tons per acre), and the Coastal Plain the least (2.4 tons per acre). CWD is classified as a 1,000-hour fuel, while fine woody debris (FWD) is classified into 1-, 10-, and 100-hour fuel categories. These fuel class numbers correspond to the approximate amount of time required for the moisture content to fluctuate within a given piece of deadwood (Brown 1974). Consequently, FWD is an important factor in fire hazard prediction. Overall, FWD biomass averaged 3.5 tons per acre. While plot values ranged from 0 to 23.5 tons per acre, 43 percent of plots had < 2.5 tons per acre. Biomass of duff, litter, and slash averaged 9.9, 3.5, and 1.1 tons per acre, respectively. CWD and FWD contributed an average of 1.4 and 1.7 tons per acre, respectively, of carbon to the ecosystem. The forest floor (duff plus litter) averaged 6.9 tons of carbon per acre.

Table 12—Fuel loadings on P3 plots by survey unit and fuel class, Virginia, 2007

		Down and dead woody fuels				Forest floor fuels			
Survey unit	plots	1-hour	10-hour	100-hour	1,000-hour	Slash	Duff	Litter	Total
	n	- tons per acre -							
Coastal Plain	38	0.2	0.9	3.0	2.4	0.2	10.7	5.1	22.7
Southern Piedmont	41	0.2	0.8	2.0	2.7	0.2	7.4	3.8	17.2
Northern Piedmont	27	0.1	0.7	2.5	2.6	4.4	10.0	3.0	23.7
Northern Mountains	28	0.2	0.8	2.5	3.5	0.8	11.1	2.5	21.5
Southern Mountains	27	0.2	0.7	2.7	3.4	0.8	11.0	2.3	21.5
Total	161	0.2	0.8	2.5	2.9	1.1	9.9	3.5	21.1

Big Cedar Creek near confluence with Clinch River, Pinnacle Natural Area Preserve, Russell County, VA. (photo by Anita K. Rose)

Abrams, M.D. 1992. Fire and the development of oak forests. Bioscience. 42(5): 346–353.

Abrams, M.D.; Copenheaver, C.A. 1999. Temporal variation in species recruitment and dendroecology of an old-growth white oak forest in the Virginia Piedmont, USA. Forest Ecology and Management. 124: 275–284.

Agren, G.I.; Bosatta, E. 1988. Nitrogen saturation of terrestrial ecosystems. Environmental Pollution. 54: 185–197.

Asaro, C. 2007. Forest health review. Virginia Department of Forestry. http://www.dof.virginia.gov/health/resources/health-review-2007-11.pdf. [Date accessed: October 27, 2008].

Bechtold, W.A.; Brown, M.J.; Tansey, J.B. 1987. Virginia's forests. Resour. Bull. SE–95. Asheville, NC: U.S. Department of Agriculture Forest Service, Southeastern Forest Experiment Station. 89 p.

Bechtold, W.A.; Patterson, P.L., eds. 2005. The enhanced forest inventory and analysis program—national sampling design and estimation procedures. Gen. Tech. Rep. SRS–80. Asheville, NC: U.S. Department of Agriculture Forest Service, Southern Research Station. 85 p.

Beven, J.; Cobb, H. 2004. Tropical cyclone report Hurricane Isabel. http://www.nhc.noaa.gov/2003isabel.shtml. [Date accessed: November 16, 2007].

Black, C.A. 1957. Soil-plant relationships. New York: John Wiley. 332 p.

Brady, N.C.; Weil, R.R. 1996. The nature and properties of soils. 11th ed. Upper Saddle River, NJ: Prentice-Hall. 740 p.

Brown, J.K. 1974. Handbook for inventorying downed woody material. Gen. Tech. Rep. INT–16. Ogden, UT: U.S. Department of Agriculture Forest Service, Intermountain Forest and Range Experiment Station. 24 p.

Burns, R.M.; Honkala, B.H., tech. coords. 1990. Silvics of North America: hardwoods. Agric. Handb. 654. Washington, DC: U.S. Department of Agriculture. 877 p. Vol. 2.

Butler, B.J.; Leatherberry, E.C.; Williams, M.S. 2005. Design, implementation, and analysis methods for the national woodland owner survey. Gen. Tech. Rep. NE–336. Newtown, PA: U.S. Department of Agriculture Forest Service, Northeastern Research Station. 43 p.

Cole, A.M.; Ware, S.W. 1997. Forest vegetation, edaphic factors, and successional direction in the central Piedmont of Virginia. Castanea. 62(2): 100–111.

Craig, R.B. 1949. Virginia forest resources and industries. Misc. Publ. 681. Washington, DC: U.S. Department of Agriculture Forest Service, Southeastern Forest Experiment Station. 64 p.

Farrell, M.M.; Ware, S. 1991. Edaphic factors and forest vegetation in the Piedmont of Virginia. Bulletin of the Torrey Botanical Club. 118(2): 161–169.

Fenneman, N.M. 1938. Physiography of Eastern United States. 1st ed. New York: McGraw Hill. 714 p.

Garten, C.T.; Van Miegroet, H. 1994. Relationships between soil nitrogen dynamics and natural 15N abundance in plant foliage from Great Smoky Mountains National Park. Canadian Journal of Forest Research. 24: 1636–1645.

Harmon, M.E.; Cromack, K., Jr.; Smith, B.G. 1987. Coarse woody debris in mixed-conifer forests, Sequoia National Park, California. Canadian Journal of Forest Research. 17: 1265–1272.

Keenan, R.J.; Prescott, C.E.; Kimmins, J.P. 1993. Mass and nutrient content of woody debris and forest floor in western red cedar and western hemlock forests on northern Vancouver Island. Canadian Journal of Forest Research. 23: 1052–1059.

Knight, H.A.; McClure, J.P. 1967. Virginia's timber, 1966. Resour. Bull. SE–8. Asheville, NC: U.S. Department of Agriculture Forest Service, Southeastern Forest Experiment Station. 47 p.

Knight, H.A.; McClure, J.P. 1978. Virginia's timber, 1977. Resour. Bull. SE–44. Asheville, NC: U.S. Department of Agriculture Forest Service, Southeastern Forest Experiment Station. 53 p.

Larson, R.W.; Bryan, M.B. 1959. Virginia's timber. For. Surv. Release 54. Asheville, NC: U.S. Department of Agriculture Forest Service, Southeastern Forest Experiment Station. 72 p.

Lovett, G.M.; Canham, C.D.; Arthur, M.A. [and others]. 2006. Forest ecosystem responses to exotic pests and pathogens in Eastern North America. BioScience. 56: 395–405.

Lundgren, M.R.; Small, C.J.; Dreyer, G.D. 2004. Influence of land use and site characteristics on invasive plant abundance in the Quinebaug Highlands of southern New England. Northeastern Naturalist. 11: 313–332.

Merriam, R.W.; Feil, E. 2002. The potential impact of an introduced shrub on native plant diversity and forest regeneration. Biological Invasions. 4: 369–373.

Miles, P.D. 2008. Forest inventory mapmaker Web-application. Version 3.0. St. Paul, MN: U.S. Department of Agriculture Forest Service, North Central Research Station. www.ncrs2. fs.fed.us/4801/fiadb/index.html. [Date accessed: November 3].

O'Neill, K.P.; Amacher, M.C.; Perry, C.H. 2005. Soils as an indicator of forest health: a guide to the collection, analysis, and interpretation of soil indicator data in the forest inventory and analysis program. Gen. Tech. Rep. NC–258. St. Paul, MN: U.S. Department of Agriculture Forest Service, North Central Research Station. 53 p.

Orr, S.P.; Rudgers, J.A.; Clay, K. 2005. Invasive plants can inhibit tree seedlings: testing potential allelopathic mechanisms. Plant Ecology. 181: 153–165.

Patterson, M.C.; Samuelson, L.; Somers, G.; Mays, A. 2000. Environmental control of stomatal conductance in forest trees of the Great Smoky Mountains National Park. Environmental Pollution. 110: 225–233.

Post, W.M.; Kwon, K.D. 2000. Soil carbon sequestration and land-use change: processes and potential. Global Change Biology. 6: 317–327.

Pritchett, W.L.; Fisher, R.F. 1987. Properties and management of forest soils. 2^d ed. New York: John Wiley. 494 p.

Randolph, K.C.; Rose, A.K. 2009. Tree crown condition in Virginia before and after Hurricane Isabel (September 2003). In: McWilliams, W.; Moisen, G.; Czaplewski, R., comps. Forest Inventory and Analysis (FIA) Symposium 2008. Proc. RMRS–P–56CD. Fort Collins, CO: U.S. Department of Agriculture Forest Service, Rocky Mountain Research Station. 11 p.

Rose, A.K. 2007. Virginia's forest, 2001. Resour. Bull. SRS–120. Asheville, NC: U.S. Department of Agriculture Forest Service, Southern Research Station. 140 p.

Rose, A.K. 2008. The status of oak and hickory regeneration in forests of Virginia. In: Jacobs, D.F.; Michler, C.H., eds. 2008. Proceedings, 16th central hardwood forest conference. Gen. Tech. Rep. NRS–P–24. Newtown Square, PA: U.S. Department of Agriculture Forest Service, Northern Research Station: 70–79.

Schlesinger, W.H. 1991. Biogeo-chemistry: an analysis of global change. San Diego: Academic Press. 443 p.

Schomaker, M.E.; Zarnoch, S.J.; Bechtold, W.A. [and others]. 2007. Crown-condition classification: a guide to data collection and analysis. Gen. Tech. Rep. SRS–102. Asheville, NC: U.S. Department of Agriculture Forest Service, Southern Research Station. 78 p.

Thompson, M.T.; Johnson, T.G. 1994. Virginia's forests, 1992. Resour. Bull. SE–151. Asheville, NC: U.S. Department of Agriculture Forest Service, Southeastern Forest Experiment Station. 103 p.

U.S. Department of Agriculture Forest Service. 1992. Forest service resource inventories: an overview. Washington, DC: U.S. Department of Agriculture Forest Service, Forest Inventory, Economics, and Recreation Research. 39 p.

U.S. Department of Agriculture Forest Service. 2004a. Forest inventory and analysis national core field guide: field data collection procedures for phase 2 plots. Version 2.0. Washington, DC. 208 p. Vol. I. Internal report. On file with: U.S. Department of Agriculture Forest Service, Forest Inventory and Analysis, 201 14th Street, Washington, DC 20250.

U.S. Department of Agriculture Forest Service. 2004b. Forest inventory and analysis national core field guide: field data collection procedures for phase 3 plots. Version 2.0. Washington, DC. 164 p. Vol. II. Internal report. On file with: U.S. Department of Agriculture Forest Service, Forest Inventory and Analysis, 201 14th Street, Washington, DC 20250.

U.S. Department of Agriculture Forest Service. 2005. Pest alert: hemlock woolly adelgid. NA–PR–09–05. Newtown Square, PA: U.S. Department of Agriculture Forest Service, Northeastern Area State and Private Forestry. 2 p.

U.S. Department of Agriculture Forest Service. 2008. Forest inventory data online. http://199.128.173.26/fido/mastf/index.html. [Date accessed: October 27].

U.S. Department of Commerce. 2004. Service assessment: Hurricane Isabel, September 18–19, 2003. http://www.weather.gov/os/assessments/pdfs/isabel.pdf. [Date accessed: October 25, 2007].

U.S. Department of Commerce, Bureau of the Census. 2000. The 2000 decennial census. Washington, DC. [Not paged].

U.S. Environmental Protection Agency. 2004. The ozone report: measuring progress through 2003. EPA 454/K–04–001. Research Triangle Park, NC: U.S. Environmental Protection Agency, Office of Air Quality Planning and Standards Emissions, Monitoring, and Analysis Division. 19 p.

Zarnoch, S.J.; Bechtold, W.A.; Stolte, K.W. 2004. Using crown condition variables as indicators of forest health. Canadian Journal of Forest Resource. 34: 1057–1070.

1,000-hour fuels. Coarse woody debris with a transect diameter ≥ 3.0 inches (7.6 cm) in diameter and ≥ 3.0 feet long (0.9 m).

100-hour fuels. Fine woody debris with a transect diameter between 1.0 and 2.9 inches (2.5 to 7.4 cm).

10-hour fuels. Fine woody debris with a transect diameter between 0.25 and 0.9 inches (0.6 to 2.3 cm).

1-hour fuels. Fine woody debris with a transect diameter < 0.24 inches (0.6 cm).

Average annual mortality. Average annual volume of trees ≥ 5.0 inches d.b.h. that died during the intersurvey period.

Average annual removals. Average annual volume of trees ≥ 5.0 inches d.b.h. removed from the inventory by harvesting, cultural operations (such as timber-stand improvement), land clearing, or changes in land use during the intersurvey period.

Average net annual growth. Average annual net change in volume of trees ≥ 5.0 inches d.b.h. in the absence of cutting (gross growth minus mortality) during the intersurvey period.

Basal area. The area in square feet of the cross section at breast height of a single tree or of all the trees in a stand, usually expressed in square feet per acre.

Bioindicator species. A tree, woody shrub, or nonwoody herbaceous species that responds to ambient levels of ozone pollution with distinctive visible foliar symptoms.

Biomass. The aboveground fresh weight of solid wood and bark in live trees 1.0 inch d.b.h. and larger from the ground to the tip of the tree. All foliage is excluded. The weight of wood and bark in lateral limbs, secondary limbs, and twigs <0.5 inch in diameter at the point of occurrence on sapling-size trees is included but is excluded on poletimber and sawtimber-size trees.

Blind check. A reinstallation of a field measurement plot done by a qualified inspection crew without production crew data on hand for the purpose of obtaining a measure of data quality. All plot-level information, and at least two subplots are fully remeasured.

Bole. That portion of a tree between a 1-foot stump and a 4-inch top d.o.b. in trees ≥5.0 inches d.b.h.

Census water. Streams, sloughs, estuaries, canals, and other moving bodies of water ≥200 feet wide, and lakes, reservoirs, ponds, and other permanent bodies of water ≥4.5 acres in area.

Coarse woody debris (CWD). Down pieces of wood leaning more than 45 degrees from vertical with a diameter of at least 3.0 inches and a length of at least 3.0 feet (decay classes 1 through 4). Decay class 5 pieces must be at least 5.0 inches in diameter, at least 5.0 inches high from the ground, and at least 3.0 feet in length.

Cold check. An inspection done either as part of the training process, or as part of the ongoing quality control (QC) program. Normally the installation crew is not present at the time of inspection and the inspector has the completed data in-hand at the time of inspection. This type of QC measurement is a "blind" measurement in that the crews do not know when or which of their plots will be remeasured by the inspection crew and cannot, therefore, alter their performance because of knowledge that the plot is a quality assurance plot.

Commercial species. Tree species currently or potentially suitable for industrial wood products.

Compacted area. Type of compaction measured as part of the soil indicator. Examples include the junction areas of skid trails, landing areas, work areas, etc.

Condition class. The combination of discrete landscape and forest attributes that identify and define, and stratify the area associated with a plot. Examples of such attributes include condition status, forest type, stand origin, stand size, owner group, reserve status, and stand density.

Crown. The part of a tree or woody plant bearing live branches or foliage.

Crown density. The amount of crown stem, branches, twigs, shoots, buds, foliage, and reproductive structures that block light penetration through the visible crown. Dead branches and dead tops are part of the crown. Live and dead branches below the live crown base are excluded. Broken or missing tops are visually reconstructed when forming this crown outline by comparing outlines of adjacent healthy trees of the same species and d.b.h.

Crown dieback. Recent mortality of branches with fine twigs, which begins at the terminal portion of a branch and proceeds toward the trunk. Dieback is only considered when it occurs in the upper and outer portions of the tree.

D.b.h. Tree diameter in inches (outside bark) at breast height (4.5 feet aboveground).

Decay class. Qualitative assessment of stage of decay (five classes) of coarse woody debris based on visual assessments of color of wood, presence/absence of twigs and branches, texture of rotten portions, and structural integrity.

Diameter class. A classification of trees based on tree d.b.h. Two-inch diameter classes are commonly used by FIA, with the even inch as the approximate midpoint for a class. For example, the 6-inch class includes trees 5.0 through 6.9 inches d.b.h.

D.o.b. (diameter outside bark). Stem diameter including bark.

Down woody material (DWM). Woody pieces of trees and shrubs that have been uprooted (no longer supporting growth) or severed from their root system, not self-supporting, and are lying on the ground [previously named down woody debris (DWD)].

Duff. A soil layer dominated by organic material derived from the decomposition of plant and animal litter and deposited on either an organic or a mineral surface. This layer is distinguished from the litter layer in that the original organic material has undergone sufficient decomposition that the source of this material, e.g., individual plant parts, can no longer be identified.

Effective cation exchange capacity (ECEC). The sum of cations that a soil can adsorb in its natural pH (expressed in units of centimoles of positive charge per kilogram of soil).

Erosion. The wearing away of the land surface by running water, wind, ice, or other geological agents.

Fine woody debris (FWD). Down pieces of wood with a diameter < 3.0 inches, not including foliage or bark fragments.

Foliage transparency. The amount of skylight visible through microholes in the live portion of the crown. Recently defoliated branches are included in foliage transparency measurements. Macroholes are excluded unless they are the result of recent defoliation. Dieback and dead branches are always excluded from the estimate. Foliage transparency is different from crown density because it emphasizes foliage and ignores stems, branches, fruits, and holes in the crown.

Forest floor. The entire thickness of organic material overlying the mineral soil, consisting of the litter and the duff (humus).

Forest land. Land at least 10 percent stocked by forest trees of any size, or formerly having had such tree cover, and not currently developed for nonforest use. The minimum area considered for classification is 1 acre. Forested strips must be at least 120 feet wide.

Forest-type group. A grouping of several detailed forest types. The grouping is based on forest types with similar physiographic and physiognomic characteristics.

Elm-ash-cottonwood. Forests in which elm, ash, or cottonwood, singly or in combination, constitute a plurality of the stocking. (Common associates include willow, sycamore, beech, and maple.)

Loblolly-shortleaf pine. Forests in which loblolly pine, shortleaf pine, or other southern yellow pines, except longleaf or slash pine, singly or in combination, constitute a plurality of the stocking. (Common associates include oak, hickory, and gum.)

Longleaf-slash pine. Forests in which longleaf or slash pine, singly or in combination, constitute a plurality of the stocking. (Common associates include oak, hickory, and gum.)

Maple-beech-birch. Forests in which maple, beech, or yellow birch, singly or in combination, constitute a plurality of the stocking. (Common associates include hemlock, elm, basswood, and white pine.)

Oak-gum-cypress. Bottomland forests in which tupelo, blackgum, sweetgum, oaks, or southern cypress, singly or in combination, constitute a plurality of the stocking, except where pines account for 25 to 50 percent of stocking, in which case the stand would be classified as oak-pine. (Common associates include cottonwood, willow, ash, elm, hackberry, and maple.)

Oak-hickory. Forests in which upland oaks or hickory, singly or in combination, constitute a plurality of the stocking, except where pines account for 25 to 50 percent, in which case the stand would be classified as oak-pine. (Common associates include yellow-poplar, elm, maple, and black walnut.)

Oak-pine. Forests in which hardwoods (usually upland oaks) constitute a plurality of the stocking but in which pines account for 25 to 50 percent of the stocking. (Common associates include gum, hickory, and yellow-poplar.)

Spruce-fir. Forests in which spruce or true firs, singly or in combination, constitute a plurality of the stocking. (Common associates include maple, birch, and hemlock.)

White-red-jack pine. Forests in which eastern white pine, red pine, or jack pine, singly or in combination, constitute a plurality of the stocking. (Common associates include hemlock, birch, and maple.)

Gross growth. Annual increase in volume of trees ≥5.0 inches d.b.h. in the absence of cutting and mortality. (Gross growth includes survivor growth, ingrowth, growth on ingrowth, growth on removals before removal, and growth on mortality before death.)

Growing-stock trees. Living trees of commercial species classified as sawtimber, poletimber, saplings, and seedlings. Trees must contain at least one 12-foot or two 8-foot logs in the saw-log portion, currently or potentially (if too small to qualify), to be classed as growing stock. The log(s) must meet dimension and merchantability standards to qualify. Trees must also have, currently or potentially, one-third of the gross board-foot volume in sound wood.

Growing-stock volume. The cubic-foot volume of sound wood in growing-stock trees at least 5.0 inches d.b.h. from a 1-foot stump to a minimum 4.0-inch top d.o.b. of the central stem.

Hardwoods. Dicotyledonous trees, usually broadleaf and deciduous.

Soft hardwoods. Hardwood species with an average specific gravity of 0.50 or less, such as gums, yellow-poplar, cottonwoods, red maple, basswoods, and willows.

Hard hardwoods. Hardwood species with an average specific gravity > 0.50 such as oaks, hard maples, hickories, and beech.

Hexagonal grid (HEX). A hexagonal grid formed from equilateral triangles for the purpose of tessellating the FIA inventory sample. Each hexagon in the base grid has an area of 5,937 acres (2402.6 ha) and contains one (phase 2) inventory plot. The base grid can be subdivided into smaller hexagons to intensify the sample.

Humus. A soil layer dominated by organic material derived from the decomposition of plant and animal litter and deposited on either an organic or a mineral surface. This layer is distinguished from the litter layer in that the original organic material has undergone sufficient decomposition that the source of this material, e.g., individual plant parts, can no longer be identified.

Land area. The area of dry land and land temporarily or partly covered by water, such as marshes, swamps, and river floodplains (omitting tidal flats below mean high tide), streams, sloughs, estuaries, and canals < 200 feet wide, and lakes, reservoirs, and ponds < 4.5 acres in area.

Lichen. An organism generally appearing to be a single small leafy, tufted or crustlike plant that consists of a fungus and an alga or cyanobacterium living in symbiotic association.

Lichen community indicator. The set of macrolichen species collected on a FIA lichen plot using standard protocols, which serves as an indicator of ecological condition, e.g., air quality or climate, of the plot.

Lichen plot. The FIA lichen plot is a circular area, total 0.935 acre (0.4 ha), with a 120-foot (36.6 m) radius centered on subplot 1, and excluding the four subplots.

Litter. Undercomposed or only partially decomposed organic material that can be readily identified, e.g., plant leaves, twigs, etc.

Live trees. All living trees. All size classes, all tree classes, and both commercial and noncommercial species are included.

Lowland hardwood. Stands that have at least 10 percent stocking with a forest type of oak-gum-cypress, elm-ash-cottonwood, palm, or other tropical.

Measurement quality objective (MQO). An estimate of the precision, bias, and completeness of data necessary to satisfy a prescribed application, e.g., Resource Planning Act. MQO describes the established tolerance for each data element. MQOs consist of two parts: a statement of the tolerance and a percentage of time when the collected data are required to be within tolerance. MQOs can only be assigned where standard methods of sampling or field measurements exist or where experience has established upper or lower bounds on precision or bias.

Mineral soil. A soil consisting predominantly of products derived from the weathering of rocks, e.g., sands, silts, and clays.

Natural pine. Stands that (1) have not been artificially regenerated, (2) are classed as a pine or other softwood forest type, and (3) have at least 10 percent stocking.

Net annual change. Increase or decrease in volume of live trees at least 5.0 inches d.b.h. Net annual change is equal to net annual growth minus average annual removals.

Noncommercial species. Tree species of typically small size, poor form, or inferior quality that normally do not develop into trees suitable for industrial wood products.

Nonforest land. Land that has never supported forests and land formerly forested where timber production is precluded by development for other uses.

Nonstocked stands. Stands < 10 percent stocked with live trees.

Oak-pine. Stands that have at least 10 percent stocking and classed as a forest type of oak-pine.

Other forest land. Forest land other than timberland and productive reserved forest land. It includes available and reserved forest land which is incapable of producing 20 cubic feet per acre per year of industrial wood under natural conditions, because of adverse site conditions such as sterile soils, dry climate, poor drainage, high elevation, steepness, or rockiness.

Ownership. The property owned by one ownership unit, including all parcels of land in the United States.

National forest land. Federal land that has been legally designated as national forests or purchase units, and other land under the administration of the Forest Service, including experimental areas and Bankhead-Jones Title III land.

Forest industry land. Land owned by companies or individuals operating primary wood-using plants.

Nonindustrial private forest land. Privately owned land excluding forest industry land.

Corporate. Owned by corporations, including incorporated farm ownerships.

Individual. All lands owned by individuals, including farm operators.

Other public. An ownership class that includes all public lands except national forests.

Miscellaneous Federal land. Federal land other than national forests.

State, county, and municipal land. Land owned by States, counties, and local public agencies or municipalities or land leased to these governmental units for 50 years or more.

Ozone (O_3). A regional, gaseous air pollutant produced primarily through sunlight-driven chemical reactions of NO_x and hydrocarbons in the atmosphere and causing foliar injury to deciduous trees, conifers, shrubs, and herbaceous species.

Ozone bioindicator site (biosite). An open area in which ozone injury to ozone-sensitive species is evaluated. The area must meet certain site selection guidelines regarding size, condition, and plant counts to be used for ozone injury evaluations in FIA.

Phase 1 (P1). FIA activities related to remote-sensing, the primary purpose of which is to label plots and obtain stratum weights for population estimates.

Phase 2 (P2). FIA activities conducted on the network of ground plots. The primary purpose is to obtain field data that enable classification and summarization of area, tree, and other attributes associated with forest land uses.

Phase 3 (P3). FIA activities conducted on a subset of P2 plots. Additional attributes related to forest health are measured on P3 plots.

Pine plantation. Stands that (1) have been artificially regenerated by planting or direct seeding, (2) are classed as a pine or other softwood forest type, and (3) have at least 10 percent stocking.

Poletimber-size trees. Softwoods 5.0 to 8.9 inches d.b.h. and hardwoods 5.0 to 10.9 inches d.b.h.

Productive-reserved forest land. Forest land sufficiently productive to qualify as timberland but withdrawn from timber utilization through statute or administrative regulation.

Quality assurance (QA). The total integrated program for ensuring that the uncertainties inherent in FIA data are known and do not exceed acceptable magnitudes, within a stated level of confidence. QA encompasses the plans, specifications, and policies affecting the collection, processing, and reporting of data. It is the system of activities designed to provide program managers and project leaders with independent assurance that total system quality control is being effectively implemented.

Quality control (QC). The routine application of prescribed field and laboratory procedures, e.g., random check cruising, periodic calibration, instrument maintenance, use of certified standards, etc., in order to reduce random and systematic errors and ensure that data are generated within known and acceptable performance limits. QC also ensures the use of qualified personnel, reliable equipment and supplies, training of personnel, good field and laboratory practices, and strict adherence to standard operating procedures.

Rotten trees. Live trees of commercial species not containing at least one 12-foot saw log, or two noncontiguous saw logs, each ≥ 8 feet, now or prospectively, primarily because of rot or missing sections, and with less than one-third of the gross board-foot tree volume in sound material.

Rough trees. Live trees of commercial species not containing at least one 12-foot saw log, or two noncontiguous saw logs, each ≥ 8 feet, now or prospectively, primarily because of roughness, poor form, splits, and cracks, and with less than one-third of the gross board-foot tree volume in sound material; and live trees of noncommercial species.

Sapling. Live trees 1.0 to 4.9 inches (2.5 to 12.5 cm) in diameter.

Saw log. A log meeting minimum standards of diameter, length, and defect, including logs at least 8 feet long, sound and straight, with a minimum diameter inside bark for softwoods of 6 inches (8 inches for hardwoods).

Saw-log portion. The part of the bole of sawtimber trees between a 1-foot stump and the saw-log top.

Sawtimber-size trees. Softwoods 9.0 inches d.b.h. and larger and hardwoods 11.0 inches d.b.h. and larger.

Sawtimber volume. Growing-stock volume in the saw-log portion of sawtimber-size trees in board feet (International 1/4-inch rule).

Seedlings. Trees < 1.0 inch d.b.h. and > 1 foot tall for hardwoods, > 6 inches tall for softwoods, and > 0.5 inch in diameter at ground level for longleaf pine.

Select red oaks. A group of several red oak species composed of cherrybark, Shumard, and northern red oaks. Other red oak species are included in the "other red oaks" group.

Select white oaks. A group of several white oak species composed of white, swamp chestnut, swamp white, chinkapin, Durand, and bur oaks. Other white oak species are included in the "other white oaks" group.

Site class. A classification of forest land in terms of potential capacity to grow crops of industrial wood based on fully stocked natural stands.

Softwoods. Coniferous trees, usually evergreen, having leaves that are needles or scalelike.

Yellow pines. Loblolly, longleaf, slash, pond, shortleaf, pitch, Virginia, sand, spruce, and Table Mountain pines.

Other softwoods. Cypress, eastern redcedar, white cedar, eastern white pine, eastern hemlock, spruce, and fir.

Soil bulk density. The mass of soil per unit volume. A measure of the ratio of pore space to solid materials in a given soil. Expressed in grams per cubic centimeter of oven dry soil.

Soil compaction. A reduction in soil pore space caused by heavy equipment or by repeated passes of light equipment that compress the soil and break down soil aggregates. Compaction disturbs the soil structure and can cause decreased tree growth, increased water runoff, and soil erosion.

Soil texture. The relative proportions of sand, silt, and clay in a soil.

Stand age. The average age of dominant and codominant trees in the stand.

Stand origin. A classification of forest stands describing their means of origin.

Planted. Planted or artificially seeded.

Natural. No evidence of artificial regeneration.

Stand-size class. A classification of forest land based on the diameter class distribution of live trees in the stand.

Sawtimber stands. Stands at least 10 percent stocked with live trees, with one-half or more of total stocking in sawtimber and poletimber trees, and with sawtimber stocking at least equal to poletimber stocking.

Poletimber stands. Stands at least 10 percent stocked with live trees, with one-half or more of total stocking in poletimber and sawtimber trees, and with poletimber stocking exceeding sawtimber stocking.

Sapling-seedling stands. Stands at least 10 percent stocked with live trees, in which saplings and seedlings account for more than one-half of total stocking.

Nonstocked stands. Stands < 10 percent stocked with live trees.

Stocking. The degree of occupancy of land by trees, measured by basal area or the number of trees in a stand and spacing in the stand, compared with a minimum standard, depending on tree size, required to fully utilize the growth potential of the land.

Density of trees and basal area per acre required for full stocking:

D.b.h. class	Trees per acre for full stocking	Basal area
inches		*square feet per acre*
Seedlings	600	—
2	560	—
4	460	—
6	340	67
8	240	84
10	155	85
12	115	90
14	90	96
16	72	101
18	60	106
20	51	111

— = not applicable.

Timberland. Forest land capable of producing at least 20 cubic feet of industrial wood per acre per year and not withdrawn from timber utilization.

Tree. Woody plant having one erect perennial stem or trunk at least 3 inches d.b.h., a more or less definitely formed crown of foliage, and a height of at least 13 feet (at maturity).

Tree grade. A classification of the saw-log portion of sawtimber trees based on: (1) the grade of the butt log or (2) the ability to produce at least one 12-foot or two 8-foot logs in the upper section of the saw-log portion. Tree grade is an indicator of quality; grade 1 is the best quality.

Upland hardwood. Stands that have at least 10 percent stocking and classed as an oak-hickory or maple-beech-birch forest type.

Vigor class. A visual assessment of the apparent crown vigor of saplings. The purpose is to separate excellent saplings with superior crowns from stressed individuals with poor crowns.

Volume of live trees. The cubic-foot volume of sound wood in live trees at least 5.0 inches d.b.h. from a 1-foot stump to a minimum 4.0-inch top d.o.b. of the central stem.

Volume of saw-log portion of sawtimber trees. The cubic-foot volume of sound wood in the saw-log portion of sawtimber trees. Volume is the net result after deductions for rot, sweep, and other defects that affect use for lumber.

Waterfall near Rose Hill, VA. (photo by Harold Jerrell, Lee County, VA, Virginia Cooperative Extension)

Inventory Methods

The Virginia 2007 inventory was a 3-phase, fixed-plot design conducted on an annual basis. P1 provides the area estimates for the inventory. P2 involves on-the-ground measurements of sample plots by field personnel. P3 is a subset of the P2 plot system where additional measurements are made by field personnel to aid in the assessment of forest health. The three phases of the sampling method are based on a hexagonal grid (HEX) design, with successive phases being sampled with less intensity. There are 16 P2 hexagons for every P3 hexagon. P2 and P3 hexagons represent about 6,000 and 96,000 acres, respectively.

Under the annual inventory system, 20 percent (one panel) of the total number of plots in a State are measured every year over a 5-year period (one cycle). Each panel of plots is selected on a subgrid which is slightly offset from the previous panel, so that each panel covers essentially the same sample area (both spatially and in intensity) as the prior panel. In the sixth year the plots that were measured in the first panel are remeasured. This marks the beginning of the next cycle of data collection. After field measurements are completed, a cycle of data is available for the 5-year report.

Phase 1

For the 2007 inventory of Virginia the P1 forest area estimate was based on classifying National Land Cover Database (NLCD) points. Stratification of forest and nonforest was performed at the unit level. For the 2001 inventory of Virginia the P1 forest area estimate was based on classifying points as either forest or nonforest on a 25-point grid that was laid over each P2 sample plot location on an aerial photo. The forest area for each county was then determined by multiplying the percentage of forested dots by the Census Bureau's estimate of all land area for that county (U.S. Department of Commerce 2000). Plot-level expansion factors were determined by dividing the number of plots into the total land area at the county level.

Because of the change to NLCD methodology with area control at the unit level, area at the county level for 2007 data will not match the published value, as did the 2001 data. In addition, the 2007 area estimates have higher sampling errors that those in 2001.

Area estimation of all lands and ownerships was based on the probability of selection of P2 plot locations. As a result, the known

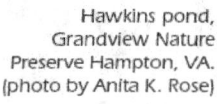

Hawkins pond, Grandview Nature Preserve Hampton, VA. (photo by Anita K. Rose)

forest land area (for specific ownerships) does not always agree with area estimates based on probability of selection. For example, the acreage of national forests, published by the National Forest System, will not agree exactly with the statistical estimate of national forest land derived by FIA. These numbers could differ substantially for very small areas.

Phase 2

Bechtold and Patterson (2005) describe P2 and P3 ground plots and explain their use. These plots are clusters of four points arranged so that one point is central and the other three lie 120 feet from it at azimuths of 0, 120, and 240 degrees (fig. A.1). Each point is the center of a circular subplot with a fixed 24-foot radius. Trees ≥ 5.0 inches in d.b.h. are measured in these subplots. Each subplot in turn contains a circular microplot with a fixed 6.8-foot radius. Trees 1.0 to 4.9 inches d.b.h. and seedlings (< 1.0 inch d.b.h.) are measured in these microplots.

Sometimes a plot cluster straddles two or more land use or forest condition classes (Bechtold and Patterson 2005). There are seven condition-class variables that require mapping of a unique condition on a plot—land use, forest type, stand size, ownership, stand density, regeneration status, and reserved status. A new condition is defined and mapped each time one of these variables changes during plot measurement.

Changes that may impact trend—The methods used to assess various attributes have changed in some cases, and this may impact trend analysis. Two of the more important attributes are forest type and stand size. Both forest type and stand size were assessed by field personnel in both the 2001 and 2007 surveys; however, figures

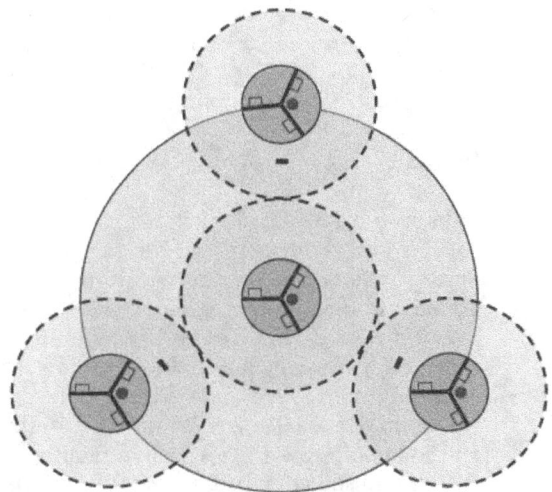

- ⬤ Subplot—24.0-foot (7.32-m) radius
- ● Microplot—6.8-foot (2.07-m) radius
- ◌ Annular plot—58.9-foot (17.95-m) radius
- ◯ Lichens plot—120.0-foot (36.60-m) radius
- ▢ Vegetation plot—1.0-m² area
- ▬ Soil sampling—(point sample)
- ━ Down woody material—24-foot (7.32-m) subplot transects

Figure A.1—Layout of fixed-radius plot.

reported here are based upon algorithms used to assign forest type and stand size by condition.

In order for there to be only one P2 plot located in each HEX cell FIA had to drop some plots from the previous survey and add some new plots. This was to ensure that the sampling intensity would be the same in all FIA regions across the United States. The 2007 survey data consist of about 77 percent remeasured plots and 23 percent new plots. This has the potential to impact trend, because the 2007 sample population is not exactly the same as in the previous survey. In addition, growth, removals, and

mortality are based on the 77 percent of plots that were remeasured, resulting in a smaller sample size for those estimates, and a potentially larger sampling error.

Phase 3

Data on forest health variables (P3) are collected on about 1/16th of the P2 sample plots. P3 data are coarse descriptions, and are meant to be used as general indicators of overall forest health over large geographic areas. P3 data collection includes variables pertaining to tree crown health, down woody material (DWM), foliar ozone injury, and soil composition. Tree crown health, DWM, and soil composition measurements are collected using the same plot design used during P2 data collection (fig. A.1).

Biomonitoring sites for ozone data collection are located independently of the FIA HEX grid. Sites must be 1-acre fields or similar open areas adjacent to or surrounded by

forest land, and must contain a minimum number of plants of at least two identified bioindicator species (U.S. Department of Agriculture Forest Service 2004b). Plants are evaluated for ozone injury, and voucher specimens are submitted to a regional expert for verification of ozone-induced foliar injury.

Summary

Users wishing to make rigorous comparisons of data between surveys should be aware of changes that occur to methodologies between measurements. The most valuable and powerful trend information is obtained when the same plots are revisited from one survey to the next and measured in the same way. Determining the strength of a trend, or determining the level of confidence associated with a trend, is difficult or impossible when sampling methods change over time.

View from Lover's Leap, Patrick County, near Vesta, VA. (photo by Anita K. Rose)

Data Reliability

A relative standard of accuracy has been incorporated into the forest survey. This standard satisfies user demands, minimizes human and instrumental sources of error, and keeps costs within prescribed limits. The two primary types of error are measurement error and sampling error.

Measurement Error

There are three elements of measurement error: (1) biased error, caused by instruments not properly calibrated; (2) compensating error, caused by instruments of moderate precision; and (3) accidental error, caused by human error in measuring and compiling. All of these are held to a minimum by the FIA quality assurance (QA) program. The goal of the QA program is to provide a framework of quality control procedures to assure the production of complete, accurate, and unbiased forest assessments for given standards. These methods include use of nationally standardized field manuals, use of portable data recorders, thorough entry-level training, periodic review training, supervision, use of check plots, editing checks, and an emphasis on careful work. Additionally, data quality is assessed and documented using performance measurements and post survey assessments. These assessments are then used to identify areas of the data collection process that need improvement or refinement in order to meet the program's quality objectives.

A stonefly nymph, an indicator of good water quality, Russell County, VA. (photo by Anita K. Rose)

Each variable collected by FIA is assigned a measurement quality objective (MQO) and a measurement tolerance level. The MQOs are documented in the FIA National Field Manual (U.S. Department of Agriculture Forest Service 2004a, 2004b). In some instances the MQOs are a "best guess" of what experienced field crews should be able to consistently achieve. Tolerances are somewhat arbitrary and are based on the ability of crews to make repeatable measurements or observations within the assigned MQO.

Evaluation of field crew performance is accomplished by calculating the differences between data collected by the field crew and that collected by the QA crew on blind check plots. Results of these calculations are compared to the established MQOs. In the analysis of blind check data, an observation is within tolerance when the difference between the field crew observation and the QA crew observation does not exceed the assigned tolerance for that variable. For many categorical variables, the tolerance is "no error" allowed, so only observations that are identical with the standard are within the tolerance level. Tables B.1 and B.2 show the percentage of observations that were within the program tolerances.

Sampling Error

Sampling error is associated with the natural and expected deviation of the sample from the true population mean. This deviation is susceptible to a mathematical evaluation of the probability of error. Sampling errors for State totals are based on one standard deviation. That is, there is a 68.27 percent probability that the confidence interval given for each sample estimate will cover the true population mean (table B.3).

Table B.1—Results of plot- and condition-level blind checks for Virginia and the southern region[a]

Variable	Virginia	Southern region	Virginia	Southern region
	percent within tolerance		*number of observations*	
Plot-level variables				
Distance to agriculture	71	67	7	136
Distance to road	86	72	7	136
Distance to urban	57	57	7	136
Latitude	100	89	7	161
Longitude	100	83	7	161
Number of accessible forest land conditions	100	96	7	136
Plot in correct county	100	100	7	172
Plot status	100	100	7	173
Sample kind	100	100	7	170
Condition-level variables				
Condition status	100	100	10	257
Reserved status	100	100	10	206
Owner group	90	99	10	206
Forest type	60	78	10	204
Forest-type group	80	86	10	204
Stand-size class	70	84	10	206
Regeneration status	100	97	10	206
Tree density	100	100	10	206
Owner class	70	96	10	206
Stand age	40	50	10	204
Disturbance 1	100	91	10	206
Treatment 1	100	93	10	206
Physiographic class	90	80	10	206
Present land use	100	98	10	206
Stand structure	80	92	10	206
Operability	80	83	10	206
Site class	90	83	10	206
Fire	100	96	10	206
Grazing	100	97	10	206

[a] Results are for data collected under manual 3.0 where available.

Table B.2—Results of tree-level blind checks for Virginia and the southern region[a]

Variable	Virginia	Southern region	Virginia	Southern region
	percent within tolerance		*number of observations*	
Azimuth	95	88	98	2,273
Board-foot cull	81	73	16	377
Cause of death	96	86	25	297
Compacted crown ratio	56	72	96	2,155
Condition number	100	97	123	2,577
Crown class	75	80	96	2,160
Decay class	100	96	11	213
Dieback incidence	100	98	67	1,398
Genus	100	99	123	2,577
Horizontal distance	100	95	98	2,271
Live d.b.h.	80	69	95	2,038
Mortality year	100	76	25	297
Present tree status	99	99	123	2,577
Reconcile	100	99	21	378
Species	100	94	123	2,577
Standing dead	100	100	11	213
Total length	86	76	21	1,485
Tree class	88	89	96	2,160
Tree grade	75	68	16	377
Utilization class	100	97	15	155

[a] Results are for data collected under manual 3.0 where available.

Table B.3—Statistical reliability for Virginia, 2007

Item	Sample estimate and 68.27 percent confidence interval	Sampling error
		percent
Forest land *(1,000 acres)*		
State	15,724.8 ± 105.4	0.7
Coastal Plain	3,701.0 ± 53.3	1.4
Southern Piedmont	3,741.7 ± 47.5	1.3
Northern Piedmont	2,502.9 ± 50.3	2.0
Northern Mountains	2,713.5 ± 36.6	1.4
Southern Mountains	3,065.6 ± 46.0	1.5
All live volume on forest land[a]		
Inventory	32,812.1 ± 436.4	1.3
Softwoods	7,530.2 ± 240.2	3.2
Hardwoods	25,281.9 ± 404.5	1.6
All live volume on timberland[a]		
Inventory	31,698.7 ± 440.6	1.4
Softwoods	7,408.6 ± 240.0	3.2
Hardwoods	24,290.1 ± 403.2	1.7
Net annual growth	1,030.4 ± 30.6	3.0
Softwoods	398.9 ± 20.5	5.1
Hardwoods	631.5 ± 22.0	3.5
Annual removals	827.5 ± 59.7	7.2
Softwoods	340.6 ± 36.2	10.6
Hardwoods	487.0 ± 39.6	8.1
Annual mortality	286.0 ± 13.1	4.6
Softwoods	96.6 ± 8.4	8.7
Hardwoods	189.3 ± 10.1	5.3

[a] Million cubic feet.

The size of the sampling error generally increases as the size of the area examined decreases. Also, as area or volume totals are stratified by forest type, species, diameter class, ownership, or other subunits, the sampling error may increase and be greatest for the smallest divisions. However, there may be instances where a smaller component does not have a proportionately larger sampling error. This can happen when the postdefined strata are more homogeneous than the larger strata, thereby having a smaller variance. For specific postdefined strata the sampling error can be calculated using the following formula. Sampling errors obtained by this method are only approximations of reliability because this process assumes constant variance across all subdivisions of totals.

$$SE_s = SE_t \frac{\sqrt{X_t}}{\sqrt{X_s}}$$

where

SE_s = sampling error for subdivision of survey unit or State total

SE_t = sampling error for survey unit or State total

X_s = sum of values for the variable of interest (area or volume) for subdivision of survey unit or State

X_t = total area or volume for survey unit or State

For example, the estimate of sampling error for softwood live-tree volume on public forest land is computed as:

$$SE_s = 3.19 \frac{\sqrt{7,530.2}}{\sqrt{1,079.5}} = 8.43$$

Thus, the sampling error is 8.43 percent, and the resulting 68.27-percent confidence interval for softwood live-tree volume on public forest land is 1,079.5 ± 91.0 million cubic feet.

Supplemental Tables

Table C.1—Land area by survey unit and land class, Virginia, 2007

Survey unit	Total land area[a]	Total forest	Forest land Timber- land	Productive reserved	Other	Other land
			thousand acres			
Coastal Plain	6,292.9	3,701.0	3,588.7	109.0	3.3	2,575.2
Southern Piedmont	5,597.4	3,741.7	3,725.6	16.1	0.0	1,871.0
Northern Piedmont	4,392.0	2,502.9	2,368.6	134.3	0.0	1,878.6
Northern Mountains	4,290.2	2,713.5	2,554.3	115.5	43.7	1,574.9
Southern Mountains	4,767.6	3,065.6	3,006.1	24.8	34.7	1,692.1
All units	25,340.1	15,724.8	15,243.3	399.8	81.8	9,591.8

Numbers in rows and columns may not sum to totals due to rounding.

0.0 = no sample for the cell or a value of > 0.0 but < 0.05.

[a] From the U.S. Bureau of the Census, 2000.

Table C.2—Area of forest land by ownership class and land status, Virginia, 2007

Ownership class	All forest land	Unreserved			Reserved		
		Total	Timber-land	Unpro-ductive	Total	Pro-ductive	Unpro-ductive
			thousand acres				
Forest Service							
National forest	1,749.5	1,694.5	1,638.7	55.8	55.0	55.0	0.0
Total	1,749.5	1,694.5	1,638.7	55.8	55.0	55.0	0.0
Other Federal							
National Park Service	217.4	0.0	0.0	0.0	217.4	217.4	0.0
U.S. Fish and Wildlife Service	82.6	5.9	5.9	0.0	76.7	76.7	0.0
Dept. of Defense/Dept. of Energy	138.2	132.2	132.2	0.0	5.9	5.9	0.0
Other Federal	93.3	93.3	93.3	0.0	0.0	0.0	0.0
Total	531.6	231.5	231.5	0.0	300.1	300.1	0.0
State and local government							
State	300.2	271.6	271.6	0.0	28.6	28.6	0.0
Local	217.2	194.7	194.7	0.0	22.4	16.2	6.2
Total	517.4	466.4	466.4	0.0	51.0	44.8	6.2
Forest industry							
Corporate	549.8	549.8	549.8	0.0	0.0	0.0	0.0
Individual	1.3	1.3	1.3	0.0	0.0	0.0	0.0
Total	551.2	551.2	551.2	0.0	0.0	0.0	0.0
Nonindustrial private							
Corporate	2,262.9	2,262.9	2,258.9	4.1	0.0	0.0	0.0
Conservation/natural resources organization	92.3	92.3	86.1	6.2	0.0	0.0	0.0
Unincorporated local partnership/association/club	113.3	113.3	113.3	0.0	0.0	0.0	0.0
Individual	9,906.7	9,906.7	9,897.2	9.5	0.0	0.0	0.0
Total	12,375.3	12,375.3	12,355.6	19.7	0.0	0.0	0.0
All classes	15,724.8	15,318.8	15,243.3	75.5	406.1	399.8	6.2

Numbers in rows and columns may not sum to totals due to rounding.
0.0 = no sample for the cell or a value of > 0.0 but < 0.05.

Table C.3—Area of forest land by forest-type group and ownership class, Virginia, 2007

Forest-type group	All ownerships	Forest Service	Other Federal	State and local government	Forest industry	Nonindustrial private
				thousand acres		
Softwood types						
White-red-jack pine	159.9	42.4	0.0	6.2	7.0	104.3
Spruce-fir	12.3	4.6	0.0	6.2	0.0	1.5
Loblolly-shortleaf pine	2,875.4	61.7	86.4	63.6	252.4	2,411.2
Pinyon-juniper[a]	108.8	0.0	0.0	7.2	0.0	101.6
Total softwoods	3,156.4	108.7	86.4	83.2	259.4	2,618.6
Hardwood types						
Oak-pine	1,606.8	150.2	63.2	59.2	46.3	1,287.9
Oak-hickory	9,807.5	1,420.5	305.9	324.3	170.0	7,586.8
Oak-gum-cypress	324.8	0.0	60.7	13.6	19.5	231.0
Elm-ash-cottonwood	358.3	0.0	0.0	24.7	27.0	306.5
Maple-beech-birch	336.3	70.0	0.0	12.4	7.7	246.2
Aspen-birch	8.0	0.0	6.4	0.0	0.0	1.6
Exotic hardwood	32.0	0.0	0.0	0.0	0.0	32.0
Total hardwoods	12,473.7	1,640.7	436.3	434.2	270.5	9,692.0
Nonstocked	94.8	0.0	8.9	0.0	21.2	64.7
All groups	15,724.8	1,749.5	531.6	517.4	551.2	12,375.3

Numbers in rows and columns may not sum to totals due to rounding.

0.0 = no sample for the cell or a value of > 0.0 but < 0.05.

[a] Pinyon-juniper includes eastern redcedar forest type.

Table C.4—Area of forest land by forest-type group and stand-size class, Virginia, 2007

Forest-type group	All size classes	Stand-size class			
		Large diameter	Medium diameter	Small diameter	Nonstocked
			thousand acres		
Softwood types					
White-red-jack pine	159.9	114.7	39.5	5.7	0.0
Spruce-fir	12.3	12.3	0.0	0.0	0.0
Loblolly-shortleaf pine	2,875.4	1,169.1	1,108.8	597.5	0.0
Pinyon-juniper[a]	108.8	19.8	42.3	46.6	0.0
Total softwoods	3,156.4	1,315.9	1,190.6	649.8	0.0
Hardwood types					
Oak-pine	1,606.8	849.1	400.9	356.8	0.0
Oak-hickory	9,807.5	6,668.7	1,884.4	1,254.4	0.0
Oak-gum-cypress	324.8	246.0	47.1	31.7	0.0
Elm-ash-cottonwood	358.3	240.1	64.7	53.5	0.0
Maple-beech-birch	336.3	271.0	34.1	31.2	0.0
Aspen-birch	8.0	0.0	1.6	6.4	0.0
Exotic hardwood	32.0	0.0	10.0	22.0	0.0
Total hardwoods	12,473.7	8,274.8	2,442.9	1,756.0	0.0
Nonstocked	94.8	0.0	0.0	0.0	94.8
All groups	15,724.8	9,590.8	3,633.5	2,405.8	94.8

Numbers in rows and columns may not sum to totals due to rounding.

0.0 = no sample for the cell or a value of > 0.0 but < 0.05.

[a] Pinyon-juniper includes eastern redcedar forest type.

Table C.5—Area of timberland by forest-type group and stand origin, Virginia, 2007

Forest-type group	Total	Stand origin	
		Natural stands	Artificial regeneration
		thousand acres	
Softwood types			
White-red-jack pine	159.9	100.5	59.4
Spruce-fir	12.3	10.8	1.5
Loblolly-shortleaf pine	2,842.4	1,068.0	1,774.4
Pinyon-juniper[a]	108.8	104.3	4.5
Total softwoods	3,123.4	1,283.7	1,839.7
Hardwood types			
Oak-pine	1,562.6	1,305.9	256.6
Oak-hickory	9,482.2	9,241.3	240.9
Oak-gum-cypress	269.9	267.0	3.0
Elm-ash-cottonwood	358.3	352.3	5.9
Maple-beech-birch	319.8	319.8	0.0
Aspen-birch	8.0	8.0	0.0
Exotic hardwood	32.0	32.0	0.0
Total hardwoods	12,032.9	11,526.4	506.5
Nonstocked	87.0	64.0	23.0
All groups	15,243.3	12,874.1	2,369.2

Numbers in rows and columns may not sum to totals due to rounding.

0.0 = no sample for the cell or a value of > 0.0 but < 0.05.

[a] Pinyon-juniper includes eastern redcedar forest type.

Table C.6—Area of forest land disturbed annually by forest-type group and disturbance class, Virginia, 2007

Forest-type group	Disturbance class							
	Insects	Disease	Weather	Fire	Domestic animals	Wild animals	Human	Other natural
					thousand acres			
Softwood types								
White-red-jack pine	10.5	0.0	0.3	0.0	0.0	1.2	1.7	0.0
Spruce-fir	1.5	0.0	0.0	0.0	0.0	0.0	0.0	0.0
Loblolly-shortleaf pine	9.8	0.0	11.0	3.4	2.6	7.2	3.9	2.4
Pinyon-juniper[a]	0.0	0.0	0.0	0.0	0.0	0.0	1.4	0.0
Total softwoods	21.8	0.0	11.3	3.4	2.6	8.5	7.1	2.4
Hardwood types								
Oak-pine	7.7	0.0	5.6	7.2	3.1	1.5	6.4	0.0
Oak-hickory	64.2	7.5	62.7	14.7	47.9	34.9	68.6	14.2
Oak-gum-cypress	0.0	0.0	8.7	0.0	0.0	3.4	0.0	0.0
Elm-ash-cottonwood	0.0	1.3	13.5	0.0	1.4	11.6	0.0	0.9
Maple-beech-birch	7.0	0.0	1.2	0.0	2.7	0.6	2.3	3.0
Aspen-birch	0.0	0.0	0.0	1.3	0.0	0.0	0.0	0.0
Exotic hardwood	0.0	0.0	0.0	0.0	0.0	0.6	0.0	0.0
Total hardwoods	78.9	8.9	91.7	23.2	55.1	52.6	77.2	18.1
Nonstocked	0.0	0.0	1.5	0.0	0.6	2.2	0.3	0.0
All groups	100.7	8.9	104.5	26.7	58.3	63.3	84.6	20.6

Numbers in columns may not sum to totals due to rounding.

0.0 = no sample for the cell or a value of > 0.0 but < 0.05.

[a] Pinyon-juniper includes eastern redcedar forest type.

Table C.7—Area of forest land treated annually by forest-type group and treatment class, Virginia, 2007

				Treatment class						
		Cutting								
Forest-type group	Total cutting	Final harvest	Partial harvest	Seed tree/ shelter- wood harvest	Com- mercial thinning	Timber stand improve- ment	Site prepa- ration	Artificial regener- ation	Natural regener- ation	Other natural
					thousand acres					
Softwood types										
White-red-jack pine	0.7	0.4	0.3	0.0	0.0	0.0	0.2	0.0	0.0	0.0
Spruce-fir	0.0	0.0	0.0	0.0	0.0	0.0	0.0	0.0	0.0	0.0
Loblolly-shortleaf pine	89.2	26.1	10.8	0.0	47.4	4.9	32.8	40.4	4.2	8.2
Pinyon-juniper[a]	1.1	1.1	0.0	0.0	0.0	0.0	1.1	1.1	0.0	0.0
Total softwoods	91.0	27.6	11.0	0.0	47.4	4.9	34.1	41.5	4.2	8.2
Hardwood types										
Oak-pine	37.7	24.9	6.0	0.0	5.6	1.2	15.5	14.6	2.8	2.4
Oak-hickory	172.4	67.3	96.2	2.6	2.0	4.3	8.8	17.8	31.8	2.8
Oak-gum-cypress	3.4	0.4	3.1	0.0	0.0	0.0	0.0	0.0	0.0	0.0
Elm-ash-cottonwood	4.8	4.8	0.0	0.0	0.0	0.0	0.0	0.0	2.9	0.0
Maple-beech-birch	3.5	1.8	1.7	0.0	0.0	0.0	0.0	0.0	0.0	0.0
Aspen-birch	0.0	0.0	0.0	0.0	0.0	0.0	0.0	0.0	0.0	0.0
Exotic hardwood	0.0	0.0	0.0	0.0	0.0	0.0	0.0	0.0	0.0	0.0
Total hardwoods	221.8	99.1	106.9	2.6	7.6	5.5	24.2	32.4	37.4	5.2
Nonstocked	6.8	6.8	0.0	0.0	0.0	0.0	1.7	0.8	0.3	0.0
All groups	319.6	133.6	117.9	2.6	55.0	10.4	60.0	74.7	41.9	13.4

Numbers in rows and columns may not sum to totals due to rounding.

0.0 = no sample for the cell or a value of > 0.0 but < 0.05.

[a] Pinyon-juniper includes eastern redcedar forest type.

Table C.8—Number of live trees on forest land by species group and diameter class, Virginia, 2007

Species group	All classes	1.0– 2.9	3.0– 4.9	5.0– 6.9	7.0– 8.9	9.0– 10.9	11.0– 12.9	13.0– 14.9	15.0– 16.9	17.0– 18.9	19.0– 20.9	21.0– 24.9	25.0– 28.9	29.0– 32.9	33.0– 36.9	37.0+
								million trees								
Softwood																
Longleaf and slash pines	0.1	0.0	0.0	0.0	0.0	0.0	0.0	0.0	0.0	0.0	0.0	0.0	0.0	0.0	0.0	0.0
Loblolly and shortleaf pines	1,096.9	377.8	241.9	179.0	150.6	79.2	37.7	15.3	8.6	3.7	1.5	1.4	0.2	0.0	0.0	0.0
Other yellow pines	527.3	239.0	120.8	58.6	45.6	32.5	18.0	8.4	3.2	0.9	0.2	0.1	0.0	0.0	0.0	0.0
Eastern white and red pines	171.1	83.5	30.5	20.0	13.3	8.1	5.7	3.8	2.2	1.7	0.8	0.8	0.5	0.1	0.0	0.0
Spruce and fir	5.6	2.3	0.9	0.3	0.7	0.2	0.4	0.3	0.2	0.1	0.1	0.1	0.0	0.0	0.0	0.0
Eastern hemlock	49.2	22.9	8.3	7.0	4.3	2.5	1.6	1.1	0.5	0.3	0.2	0.3	0.1	0.0	0.0	0.0
Cypress	3.4	2.2	0.0	0.1	0.2	0.1	0.1	0.1	0.1	0.1	0.2	0.0	0.0	0.0	0.0	0.0
Other eastern softwoods	250.2	168.3	44.6	20.0	9.4	4.4	1.9	1.0	0.4	0.1	0.1	0.0	0.0	0.0	0.0	0.0
Total softwoods	2,103.7	896.0	446.9	285.0	224.0	127.1	65.4	29.9	15.4	7.0	3.1	2.7	0.9	0.2	0.0	0.0
Hardwood																
Select white oaks	450.2	208.4	80.3	39.3	33.6	23.9	21.2	14.4	12.2	7.7	4.1	3.5	1.0	0.2	0.2	0.1
Select red oaks	151.4	64.8	17.5	13.9	12.4	10.8	7.3	6.4	6.0	3.5	2.6	4.0	1.1	0.4	0.3	0.2
Other white oaks	395.5	113.4	64.4	53.6	48.4	37.1	26.4	20.1	12.4	8.5	4.9	4.1	1.8	0.3	0.3	0.1
Other red oaks	558.0	308.6	78.7	45.0	35.2	28.6	20.0	15.5	10.3	6.6	4.1	3.8	1.1	0.4	0.1	0.0
Hickory	418.7	238.9	66.5	38.4	26.1	17.9	12.0	8.3	5.4	2.7	1.2	1.0	0.3	0.0	0.0	0.0
Yellow birch	12.7	7.2	2.3	0.9	0.7	0.6	0.5	0.3	0.1	0.0	0.0	0.0	0.0	0.0	0.0	0.0
Hard maple	170.8	112.1	27.8	11.4	7.4	4.4	2.8	1.9	1.4	0.7	0.3	0.4	0.0	0.1	0.0	0.0
Soft maple	1,423.5	956.4	237.5	97.8	56.8	30.8	18.8	10.4	6.6	4.1	1.6	1.9	0.6	0.3	0.0	0.0
Beech	214.8	137.8	37.9	14.0	7.9	5.5	3.4	2.8	1.8	1.3	0.8	1.0	0.5	0.1	0.0	0.0
Sweetgum	682.1	453.6	130.6	43.9	22.1	12.4	8.2	5.0	3.1	1.6	0.7	0.7	0.2	0.0	0.0	0.0
Tupelo and blackgum	655.8	482.4	104.9	32.4	14.7	9.1	5.0	3.3	1.6	1.2	0.5	0.5	0.2	0.0	0.0	0.0
Ash	177.6	106.6	26.6	15.9	10.3	6.2	5.0	3.0	1.6	1.2	0.5	0.4	0.2	0.1	0.0	0.0
Cottonwood and aspen	16.7	11.2	3.1	0.9	0.8	0.2	0.2	0.0	0.1	0.1	0.0	0.0	0.0	0.0	0.0	0.0
Basswood	23.6	10.4	3.1	2.6	2.2	1.3	1.1	1.1	0.7	0.5	0.4	0.2	0.0	0.0	0.0	0.0
Yellow-poplar	846.5	496.2	120.9	66.0	42.2	31.6	25.3	21.5	16.0	10.6	7.3	6.0	1.9	0.7	0.2	0.1
Black walnut	18.8	5.5	2.7	3.1	1.9	1.7	1.6	1.0	0.7	0.3	0.2	0.1	0.1	0.0	0.0	0.0
Other eastern soft hardwoods	695.4	470.8	121.4	42.7	23.7	14.7	8.8	5.4	3.3	2.3	1.0	0.7	0.2	0.2	0.1	0.0
Other eastern hard hardwoods	1,004.8	773.3	145.2	42.2	19.8	11.2	6.1	3.5	1.6	0.7	0.6	0.4	0.2	0.0	0.0	0.0
Eastern noncommercial hardwoods	1,132.4	863.1	186.8	51.1	20.4	7.0	2.3	1.1	0.6	0.0	0.0	0.0	0.0	0.0	0.0	0.0
Total hardwoods	9,049.3	5,820.6	1,458.1	615.3	386.8	254.9	175.8	124.9	85.7	53.8	30.9	28.6	9.4	2.6	1.2	0.6
All species	11,153.0	6,716.7	1,905.1	900.3	610.8	382.0	241.2	154.8	101.0	60.8	34.0	31.2	10.4	2.9	1.2	0.6

Numbers in rows and columns may not sum to totals due to rounding.

0.0 = no sample for the cell or a value of > 0.0 but < 0.05.

Table C.9—Volume of live trees on forest land by species group and ownership class, Virginia, 2007

Species group	All ownerships	Forest Service	Other Federal	State and local government	Forest industry	Nonindustrial private
				million cubic feet		
Softwood						
Longleaf and slash pines	0.7	0.0	0.0	0.0	0.0	0.7
Loblolly and shortleaf pines	4,494.4	5.5	198.4	127.3	364.1	3,799.0
Other yellow pines	1,767.1	220.2	92.8	62.2	34.8	1,357.1
Eastern white and red pines	777.9	222.5	17.2	9.4	19.9	508.9
Spruce and fir	45.3	22.2	0.0	12.9	0.0	10.2
Eastern hemlock	189.4	51.4	1.1	7.3	1.9	127.7
Cypress	54.4	0.0	3.4	0.1	2.7	48.2
Other eastern softwoods	201.1	0.0	15.0	10.6	0.9	174.7
Total softwoods	7,530.2	521.8	327.9	229.8	424.3	6,026.4
Hardwood						
Select white oaks	3,099.4	248.5	81.2	121.9	34.2	2,613.5
Select red oaks	1,685.5	466.3	118.7	62.2	25.2	1,013.0
Other white oaks	3,159.9	1,111.9	94.3	90.0	53.2	1,810.5
Other red oaks	2,849.2	415.7	106.9	82.0	54.9	2,189.7
Hickory	1,528.8	115.7	53.2	57.1	17.8	1,284.9
Yellow birch	36.4	21.0	0.0	1.9	4.5	9.0
Hard maple	390.6	88.7	4.5	18.5	11.6	267.3
Soft maple	2,253.8	240.3	187.7	101.9	41.8	1,682.0
Beech	570.4	10.4	9.5	33.5	12.9	504.0
Sweetgum	1,115.0	0.0	109.5	32.5	25.2	947.8
Tupelo and blackgum	600.1	46.3	44.9	36.0	25.4	447.5
Ash	566.0	26.7	34.4	36.5	8.4	460.0
Cottonwood and aspen	27.8	0.0	1.0	0.0	0.0	26.8
Basswood	199.5	53.9	19.6	22.8	4.4	98.7
Yellow-poplar	5,018.2	276.8	197.4	165.8	77.1	4,301.1
Black walnut	133.3	0.7	0.1	4.6	1.6	126.3
Other eastern soft hardwoods	1,087.4	72.5	37.6	56.2	33.0	888.2
Other eastern hard hardwoods	629.1	82.0	27.5	21.5	7.6	490.5
Eastern noncommercial hardwoods	331.6	39.9	5.4	10.1	10.2	265.9
Total hardwoods	25,281.9	3,317.4	1,133.4	955.3	449.0	19,426.8
All species	32,812.1	3,839.2	1,461.3	1,185.1	873.3	25,453.3

Numbers in rows and columns may not sum to totals due to rounding.

0.0 = no sample for the cell or a value of > 0.0 but < 0.05.

Table C.10—Volume of live trees on timberland by survey unit and species group, Virginia, 2007

| Survey unit | All species | Softwoods | | | Hardwoods | | |
		All softwood	Yellow pine	Other softwood	All hardwood	Soft hardwood	Hard hardwood
				million cubic feet			
Coastal Plain	7,479.2	2,934.5	2,872.6	61.9	4,544.8	2,419.0	2,125.8
Southern Piedmont	7,075.8	2,223.3	2,174.2	49.1	4,852.5	2,417.9	2,434.6
Northern Piedmont	5,562.2	837.8	767.9	69.9	4,724.4	1,967.1	2,757.3
Northern Mountains	5,127.3	780.2	672.8	107.4	4,347.1	880.5	3,466.6
Southern Mountains	6,454.0	632.8	453.3	179.6	5,821.2	2,183.7	3,637.4
All units	31,698.5	7,408.6	6,940.7	467.8	24,289.9	9,868.1	14,421.8

Numbers in rows and columns may not sum to totals due to rounding.

Table C.11—Total carbon of live trees on forest land by ownership class and land status, Virginia, 2007[a]

Ownership class	All forest land	Unreserved			Reserved		
		Total	Timber-land	Unpro-ductive	Total	Pro-ductive	Unpro-ductive
				thousand tons			
Forest Service							
National forest	53,467.0	51,572.7	50,184.8	1,388.0	1,894.3	1,894.3	0.0
Total	53,467.0	51,572.7	50,184.8	1,388.0	1,894.3	1,894.3	0.0
Other Federal							
National Park Service	6,723.0	0.0	0.0	0.0	6,723.0	6,723.0	0.0
U.S. Fish and Wildlife Service	2,918.5	171.5	171.5	0.0	2,747.0	2,747.0	0.0
Dept. of Defense/Dept. of Energy	5,684.5	5,383.8	5,383.8	0.0	300.7	300.7	0.0
Other Federal	3,547.1	3,547.1	3,547.1	0.0	0.0	0.0	0.0
Total	18,873.0	9,102.4	9,102.4	0.0	9,770.6	9,770.6	0.0
State and local government							
State	9,903.3	8,818.6	8,818.6	0.0	1,084.7	1,084.7	0.0
Local	5,910.1	5,263.4	5,263.4	0.0	646.6	574.7	72.0
Total	15,813.4	14,082.0	14,082.0	0.0	1,731.4	1,659.4	72.0
Forest industry							
Corporate	11,945.4	11,945.4	11,945.4	0.0	0.0	0.0	0.0
Individual	7.2	7.2	7.2	0.0	0.0	0.0	0.0
Total	11,952.6	11,952.6	11,952.6	0.0	0.0	0.0	0.0
Nonindustrial private							
Corporate	62,811.1	62,811.1	62,810.3	0.7	0.0	0.0	0.0
Conservation/organization natural resources	2,342.3	2,342.3	2,182.2	160.2	0.0	0.0	0.0
Unincorporated local partnership/association/club	2,932.1	2,932.1	2,932.1	0.0	0.0	0.0	0.0
Individual	276,636.7	276,636.7	276,541.1	95.6	0.0	0.0	0.0
Total	344,722.3	344,722.3	344,465.7	256.5	0.0	0.0	0.0
All classes	444,828.2	431,431.9	429,787.4	1,644.5	13,396.3	13,324.3	72.0

Numbers in rows and columns may not sum to totals due to rounding.

0.0 = no sample for the cell or a value of > 0.0 but < 0.05.

[a] Estimates of carbon calculated by multiplying aboveground dry tree biomass by 0.5.

Table C.12—Average annual net growth of live trees by ownership class and land status, Virginia, 2002 to 2007

Ownership class	Timberland	Forest land
	million cubic feet	
Forest Service		
National forest	43.5	40.6
Total	43.5	40.6
Other Federal		
National Park Service	-0.1	2.7
U.S. Fish and Wildlife Service	-0.1	2.4
Dept. of Defense/Dept. of Energy	7.3	7.6
Other Federal	9.9	9.9
Total	17.1	22.6
State and local government		
State	11.1	12.3
Local	17.1	17.1
Total	28.2	29.4
Forest industry		
Corporate	50.8	50.8
Individual	0.1	0.1
Total	50.9	50.9
Nonindustrial private		
Corporate	189.0	189.0
Unincorporated partnership/ association/club	5.6	5.6
Individual	692.1	692.1
Conservation/natural resources organization	3.9	3.9
Total	890.7	890.7
All classes	1,030.4	1,034.2

Numbers in columns may not sum to totals due to rounding.

Table C.13—Average annual mortality of live trees by ownership class and land status, Virginia, 2002 to 2007

Ownership class	Timberland	Forest land
	million cubic feet	
Forest Service		
National forest	28.4	28.4
Total	28.4	28.4
Other Federal		
National Park Service	0.1	4.2
U.S. Fish and Wildlife Service	0.3	1.9
Dept. of Defense/Dept. of Energy	5.1	5.4
Other Federal	2.3	2.3
Total	7.7	13.8
State and local government		
State	8.1	8.2
Local	3.7	4.3
Total	11.8	12.5
Forest industry		
Corporate	7.8	7.8
Total	7.8	7.8
Nonindustrial private		
Corporate	40.6	40.6
Unincorporated partnership/ association/club	1.9	1.9
Individual	186.3	186.3
Conservation/natural resources organization	1.5	1.5
Total	230.2	230.2
All classes	286.0	292.8

Numbers in columns may not sum to totals due to rounding.

Table C.14—Average annual removals of live trees by ownership class and land status, Virginia, 2002 to 2007

Ownership class	Timberland	Forest land
	million cubic feet	
Forest Service		
National forest	21.6	14.0
Total	21.6	14.0
Other Federal		
National Park Service	1.4	0.0
U.S. Fish and Wildlife Service	5.9	0.0
Dept. of Defense/Dept. of Energy	6.3	6.3
Other Federal	5.6	5.6
Total	19.1	11.8
State and local government		
State	2.3	2.3
Local	14.0	12.9
Total	16.3	15.2
Forest industry		
Corporate	65.0	65.0
Total	65.0	65.0
Nonindustrial private		
Corporate	150.4	150.4
Unincorporated partnership/ association/club	0.9	0.9
Individual	553.5	553.5
Conservation/natural resources organization	0.6	0.6
Total	705.4	705.4
All classes	827.5	811.4

Numbers in columns may not sum to totals due to rounding.

0.0 = no sample for the cell or a value of > 0.0 but < 0.05.

Table C.15—Area of land by county and condition status, Virginia, 2007

County	FIPS code	Accessible forest Area (thousand acres)	SE (percent)	Nonforest Area (thousand acres)	SE (percent)	Noncensus water Area (thousand acres)	SE (percent)	Census water Area (thousand acres)	SE (percent)	Denied access Area (thousand acres)	SE (percent)	Total Area (thousand acres)	SE (percent)
Accomack	1	107.9	22.6	212.4	15.7	7.3	90.1	574.7	8.6			902.3	7.1
Albemarle	3	279.9	13.5	205.9	15.7	3.9	62.8			1.6	96.6	491.3	10.4
Alleghany	5	231.1	15.2	48.4	32.2	1.3	124.8					280.8	14.1
Amelia	7	152.9	18.8	67.2	27.8	2.9	102.3			1.5	101.1	224.4	16.0
Amherst	9	231.6	15.0	69.1	26.0							300.7	13.6
Appomattox	11	125.3	20.3	87.4	23.9	2.2	101.1					214.9	16.4
Arlington	13			16.9	59.1							16.9	59.1
Augusta	15	325.3	12.4	305.3	12.2							630.6	8.9
Bath	17	315.3	12.9	41.3	36.3			4.8	124.8			361.4	12.1
Bedford	19	288.1	13.3	188.3	16.1	5.7	102.3	8.6	78.1			490.7	10.6
Bland	21	173.6	17.8	69.5	27.9							243.1	15.3
Botetourt	23	240.3	15.0	101.7	23.0			4.9	122.0	6.2	98.0	353.1	12.4
Brunswick	25	269.6	14.2	91.0	24.1					5.5	90.1	366.2	12.4
Buchanan	27	284.5	13.5	48.5	28.3							333.0	12.9
Buckingham	29	320.0	12.8	49.5	29.4	1.4	100.3			5.7	102.3	376.6	12.1
Campbell	31	209.4	16.0	144.3	18.7	1.5	100.3			5.9	100.3	361.1	12.4
Caroline	33	244.9	14.7	83.0	24.5	1.8	100.7			5.2	107.5	334.9	12.9
Carroll	35	183.1	16.3	134.7	18.6	1.4	105.0	5.4	105.0			324.6	13.1
Charles City	36	91.6	24.3	37.2	36.4			7.7	85.7			136.5	20.7
Charlotte	37	215.9	15.7	79.4	24.0							295.3	13.9
Chesterfield	41	164.7	17.8	135.8	19.5	1.7	85.7	10.5	66.4			312.7	13.5
Clarke	43	24.7	46.7	87.5	25.1							112.1	22.6
Craig	45	153.3	18.9	43.0	35.1	6.4	96.6					196.3	17.0
Culpeper	47	109.7	22.4	120.7	21.1							236.7	15.4
Cumberland	49	114.4	22.0	65.5	28.6	4.4	100.3	7.1	91.8	5.8	101.1	197.3	17.0
Dickenson	51	196.6	16.5	40.2	33.1					1.6	90.8	238.5	15.4
Dinwiddie	53	223.9	15.6	73.8	26.7	1.0	107.5			5.9	100.7	304.6	13.6
Essex	57	79.7	26.4	76.4	27.0			7.3	90.1			163.5	18.9
Fairfax	59	95.7	23.9	178.9	17.3							274.6	14.2
Fauquier	61	203.2	16.1	218.1	15.2					5.5	103.8	426.9	11.2
Floyd	63	120.5	21.2	120.0	21.3							240.5	15.4
Fluvanna	65	99.7	22.5	56.0	29.0			6.2	102.7			161.9	18.8
Franklin	67	264.6	13.8	190.9	16.3			4.4	75.1			459.9	10.9
Frederick	69	154.7	18.6	110.7	21.7							265.4	14.6

continued

Table C.15—Area of land by county and condition status, Virginia, 2007 (continued)

County	FIPS code	Accessible forest Area (thousand acres)	SE (percent)	Nonforest Area (thousand acres)	SE (percent)	Noncensus water Area (thousand acres)	SE (percent)	Census water Area (thousand acres)	SE (percent)	Denied access Area (thousand acres)	SE (percent)	Total Area (thousand acres)	SE (percent)
Giles	71	190.1	16.8	51.0	32.4			5.7	102.6			246.8	15.0
Gloucester	73	88.7	25.0	39.4	36.5	7.3	90.1	57.0	32.0			192.5	17.4
Goochland	75	108.7	22.3	64.3	28.7			1.6	96.6			174.6	18.1
Grayson	77	158.8	17.9	119.5	20.4	1.5	100.6	5.7	102.6			285.4	14.0
Greene	79	73.1	27.2	35.3	38.6	1.5	96.6					109.9	23.0
Greensville	81	122.2	21.3	38.2	37.8	5.7	79.6					166.1	18.7
Halifax	83	360.9	12.0	160.8	17.7			7.1	91.8			528.8	10.1
Hanover	85	182.3	17.0	96.6	22.8			1.3	107.5			280.2	14.3
Henrico	87	57.9	29.5	115.3	22.0	3.9	76.1			2.2	98.4	179.3	18.0
Henry	89	190.7	16.9	71.4	27.3			4.4	100.3			266.6	14.6
Highland	91	222.6	15.7	70.1	28.0							292.7	13.8
Isle of Wight	93	106.3	22.5	103.6	22.7	5.2	107.5	7.3	90.1			222.4	16.1
James City	95	63.2	29.3	46.8	33.4			14.7	63.6			124.6	21.7
King and Queen	97	136.5	20.1	57.7	30.0			5.9	100.7			200.1	17.0
King George	99	73.7	27.1	28.9	41.2			5.9	100.7			108.4	23.2
King William	101	103.3	22.7	65.6	27.9			7.3	90.1			176.2	18.2
Lancaster	103	44.4	33.2	51.8	31.1	1.5	98.4	36.7	40.0			134.5	20.9
Lee	105	176.5	17.5	105.7	22.3					2.9	71.9	285.1	14.1
Loudoun	107	119.8	21.0	219.7	15.3	2.2	76.2					341.7	12.6
Louisa	109	192.6	16.4	115.8	20.8	3.2	96.6	17.3	55.9	6.4	96.6	335.3	12.8
Lunenburg	111	232.2	15.3	47.5	32.2							279.7	14.2
Madison	113	93.7	24.6	101.1	23.6							194.9	17.1
Mathews	115	24.7	46.4	21.1	49.7			130.1	20.7			175.8	18.0
Mecklenburg	117	292.4	13.4	129.8	19.7			14.3	62.2			436.5	11.3
Middlesex	119	52.6	32.7	39.9	37.2	5.2	107.5	34.6	41.3			132.2	21.1
Montgomery	121	161.3	18.5	99.3	23.5							260.6	14.7
Nelson	125	252.5	14.5	46.7	33.9							299.2	13.5
New Kent	127	83.3	25.5	23.1	46.1	8.6	78.3	3.9	107.5			119.0	22.2
Northampton	131	25.7	46.1	140.2	19.6			408.4	10.8			574.3	9.3
Northumberland	133	57.1	30.3	66.4	28.3			69.4	29.0			192.9	17.4
Nottoway	135	138.2	20.0	58.1	29.8					5.8	101.1	202.2	16.9
Orange	137	136.2	19.7	82.9	24.8	1.7	87.5	6.2	102.7			227.0	15.8
Page	139	100.9	23.6	73.9	27.3			4.8	124.8			179.6	17.9
Patrick	141	199.8	16.5	87.4	24.8	5.9	100.3	1.7	100.3			294.8	13.9

continued

Table C.15—Area of land by county and condition status, Virginia, 2007 (continued)

County	FIPS code	Accessible forest Area thousand acres	SE percent	Nonforest Area thousand acres	SE percent	Noncensus water Area thousand acres	SE percent	Census water Area thousand acres	SE percent	Denied access Area thousand acres	SE percent	Total Area thousand acres	SE percent
Pittsylvania	143	375.9	11.5	272.5	13.0	0.3	100.3	7.1	91.8			655.7	8.9
Powhatan	145	96.4	23.2	72.1	26.5	1.5	100.3	7.1	91.8			177.1	18.1
Prince Edward	147	146.4	19.5	66.7	28.3			5.7	102.3			218.8	16.2
Prince George	149	106.3	22.6	71.5	27.7	4.6	98.4	8.6	78.3			191.1	17.4
Prince William	153	85.4	24.9	119.1	21.2			18.9	55.6			223.3	16.0
Pulaski	155	115.1	21.4	89.1	23.9			5.7	102.6			209.9	16.5
Rappahannock	157	134.5	20.3	62.9	29.8							197.4	17.0
Richmond	159	78.2	26.8	49.7	33.1			22.0	51.8			149.9	19.8
Roanoke	161	85.8	24.9	118.4	21.2							204.2	16.7
Rockbridge	163	259.0	14.2	141.8	19.1					6.2	98.0	407.0	11.6
Rockingham	165	322.9	12.6	222.7	14.9	1.8	99.5			1.6	98.0	549.0	9.7
Russell	167	144.8	19.5	142.8	19.4					3.1	69.7	290.6	13.9
Scott	169	246.8	14.7	86.5	25.4	1.5	100.6	5.7	102.6	3.0	70.4	343.5	12.7
Shenandoah	171	185.9	17.0	142.5	19.1	1.3	100.6			1.5	99.5	331.2	12.9
Smyth	173	189.0	17.0	92.7	23.9							281.8	14.2
Southampton	175	239.5	14.9	112.5	21.4	1.6	96.6	7.3	90.1			359.4	12.5
Spotsylvania	177	141.5	19.5	95.9	23.8			12.5	67.9			251.5	15.0
Stafford	179	125.5	20.4	43.8	31.7					11.1	73.3	180.4	17.8
Surry	181	142.2	19.8	25.4	43.9	3.9	107.5	22.0	51.8			193.5	17.3
Sussex	183	258.1	14.6	61.3	29.4							319.4	13.2
Tazewell	185	226.7	15.4	84.8	24.7			1.5	100.6	5.9	100.6	318.9	13.2
Warren	187	77.3	26.0	62.2	28.7							139.5	20.4
Washington	191	208.1	16.0	151.5	18.8	1.5	98.7	9.3	73.0	9.0	74.3	370.1	12.2
Westmoreland	193	88.0	24.6	57.1	30.2							154.4	19.5
Wise	195	161.9	17.9	78.3	24.7	0.4	100.6			1.5	100.6	242.1	15.2
Wythe	197	106.1	23.1	159.5	17.9	5.9	100.6			1.5	98.7	273.0	14.1
York	199	46.5	33.1	39.1	36.2			120.2	21.4			205.8	16.7
Chesapeake	550	93.0	24.6	151.7	18.9	6.2	98.4	48.0	35.0	11.8	71.1	310.7	13.5
Hampton	650	1.2	107.5	43.5	36.4			44.1	36.4			88.8	25.7
Newport News	700	5.9	100.7	39.1	38.9			29.4	44.8			74.4	28.2
Suffolk	800	175.3	17.6	75.1	26.6			21.6	51.0			272.1	14.5
Virginia Beach	810	35.9	38.4	137.0	20.2			163.1	18.2	5.9	100.7	341.9	12.8
All		15,623.2	0.7	9,442.6	1.1	126.9	18.1	2,053.0	1.9	129.8	19.7	27,375.4	0.0

FIPS = Federal Information Processing Standards; SE = sampling error.

Table C.16—Area of timberland by county and ownership class, Virginia, 2007

County	FIPS code	National forest Area (thousand acres)	National forest SE (percent)	U.S. Fish and Wildlife Service Area (thousand acres)	U.S. Fish and Wildlife Service SE (percent)	Department of Defense or Energy Area (thousand acres)	Department of Defense or Energy SE (percent)	Other Federal Area (thousand acres)	Other Federal SE (percent)	State Area (thousand acres)	State SE (percent)	Local (county, municipal, etc.) Area (thousand acres)	Local (county, municipal, etc.) SE (percent)	Undifferentiated private Area (thousand acres)	Undifferentiated private SE (percent)	Total Area (thousand acres)	Total SE (percent)
Accomack	1													103.9	23.2	103.9	23.2
Albemarle	3									1.6	96.6	4.2	103.5	264.3	14.0	270.1	13.7
Alleghany	5	120.0	21.6											99.9	23.3	219.9	15.6
Amelia	7													153.6	18.8	153.6	18.8
Amherst	9	42.6	36.7							11.8	71.2	11.2	73.1	171.2	17.5	225.0	15.2
Appomattox	11											3.4	102.2	110.7	21.6	125.9	20.3
Arlington	13																
Augusta	15	189.3	17.0							3.8	97.9			121.3	19.9	314.4	12.6
Bath	17	171.8	18.0							6.2	97.9			114.0	22.0	292.1	13.5
Bedford	19	17.6	58.2											267.6	13.8	285.2	13.3
Bland	21	96.9	24.2											76.2	27.0	173.1	17.8
Botetourt	23	78.7	26.9									4.4	97.9	145.9	19.5	229.0	15.4
Brunswick	25					7.7	81.0			6.7	85.9			255.2	14.7	269.7	14.3
Buchanan	27											5.7	102.8	281.1	13.6	286.8	13.5
Buckingham	29									23.1	50.4			298.4	13.3	321.6	12.8
Campbell	31													210.5	16.0	210.5	16.0
Caroline	33					50.3	33.1							196.5	16.6	246.8	14.7
Carroll	35	6.2	98.9							3.1	98.6			178.7	16.5	184.9	16.3
Charles City	36													89.2	24.9	92.3	24.3
Charlotte	37													216.9	15.7	216.9	15.7
Chesterfield	41									9.8	74.1	11.6	63.4	144.5	19.1	165.9	17.7
Clarke	43													24.8	46.7	24.8	46.7
Craig	45	118.5	22.0											35.6	38.3	154.2	18.9
Culpeper	47													110.4	22.3	110.4	22.3
Cumberland	49									17.6	58.2			97.4	23.9	115.0	22.0
Dickenson	51	17.7	58.2											180.5	17.3	198.2	16.5
Dinwiddie	53									1.3	107.5			224.3	15.7	225.6	15.6
Essex	57											1.2	100.4	77.6	26.8	78.8	26.4
Fairfax	59									5.6	103.5	16.8	59.6	61.9	29.3	84.3	25.4
Fauquier	61									12.0	70.6	5.6	103.5	187.1	16.8	204.7	16.0
Floyd	63													121.2	21.2	121.2	21.2
Fluvanna	65													100.6	22.4	100.6	22.4
Franklin	67									4.5	100.3			261.5	14.0	265.9	13.8
Frederick	69													155.4	18.6	155.4	18.6

continued

Table C.16—Area of timberland by county and ownership class, Virginia, 2007 (continued)

County	FIPS code	National forest Area (thousand acres)	National forest SE (percent)	U.S. Fish and Wildlife Service Area (thousand acres)	U.S. Fish and Wildlife Service SE (percent)	Department of Defense or Energy Area (thousand acres)	Department of Defense or Energy SE (percent)	Other Federal Area (thousand acres)	Other Federal SE (percent)	State Area (thousand acres)	State SE (percent)	Local (county, municipal, etc.) Area (thousand acres)	Local (county, municipal, etc.) SE (percent)	Undifferentiated private Area (thousand acres)	Undifferentiated private SE (percent)	Total Area (thousand acres)	Total SE (percent)
Giles	71	72.3	28.2									6.2	98.9	100.3	23.6	178.7	17.5
Gloucester	73													89.3	25.0	89.3	25.0
Goochland	75													109.5	22.2	109.5	22.2
Grayson	77	23.1	50.2							6.2	98.9	2.0	105.2	124.3	20.2	155.6	18.1
Greene	79													57.0	30.7	57.0	30.7
Greensville	81													123.0	21.3	123.0	21.3
Halifax	83					5.9	101.0	10.5	71.7					346.3	12.3	362.7	12.0
Hanover	85													183.5	17.0	183.5	17.0
Henrico	87									5.9	100.4	11.1	73.4	37.9	35.8	55.0	30.7
Henry	89									1.5	100.3			184.3	17.3	185.8	17.2
Highland	91	79.4	26.9							15.9	58.4			116.1	22.3	211.3	16.1
Isle of Wight	93													107.1	22.4	107.1	22.4
James City	95									5.9	100.4	5.2	107.5	52.5	31.9	63.6	29.2
King and Queen	97											5.9	100.4	131.7	20.5	137.6	20.0
King George	99							5.9	100.4					68.4	28.2	74.4	27.1
King William	101									4.1	107.5			99.9	23.2	104.0	22.7
Lancaster	103											1.4	105.4	43.3	34.0	44.6	33.1
Lee	105	18.3	57.3							12.2	70.4			147.3	19.2	177.8	17.5
Loudoun	107											5.6	103.5	115.1	21.4	120.7	21.0
Louisa	109									0.5	96.6			193.5	16.4	194.0	16.4
Lunenburg	111													233.4	15.3	233.4	15.3
Madison	113													66.4	29.5	66.4	29.5
Mathews	115													24.9	46.3	24.9	46.3
Mecklenburg	117							56.7	30.8					237.2	15.0	293.8	13.4
Middlesex	119											5.2	107.5	47.8	34.3	53.0	32.6
Montgomery	121	24.6	49.2							5.2	100.2			120.3	21.6	150.1	19.3
Nelson	125	23.2	50.7							5.6	103.5			226.0	15.4	254.8	14.4
New Kent	127											4.1	107.5	79.8	26.3	83.9	25.5
Northampton	131													25.8	46.1	25.8	46.1
Northumberland	133													57.5	30.2	57.5	30.2
Nottoway	135					11.8	71.2							127.1	20.9	138.9	20.0
Orange	137											5.6	103.5	131.6	20.0	137.2	19.6
Page	139	12.5	69.1									3.3	100.8	61.1	30.8	76.8	27.1
Patrick	141									15.8	58.7			179.2	17.5	194.9	16.7

continued

Table C.16—Area of timberland by county and ownership class, Virginia, 2007 (continued)

County	FIPS code	National forest		U.S. Fish and Wildlife Service		Department of Defense or Energy		Other Federal		State		Local (county, municipal, etc.)		Undifferentiated private		Total	
		Area thousand acres	SE percent	Area thousand acres	SE percent	Area thousand acres	SE percent	Area thousand acres	SE percent	Area thousand acres	SE percent	Area thousand acres	SE percent	Area thousand acres	SE percent	Area thousand acres	SE percent
Pittsylvania	143													377.6	11.5	377.6	11.5
Powhatan	145									0.8	101.0			96.1	23.4	96.9	23.2
Prince Edward	147									4.4	101.0	8.9	75.2	133.8	20.5	147.1	19.5
Prince George	149					1.5	100.4							105.7	22.9	107.2	22.6
Prince William	153					16.8	59.6					5.6	103.5	48.0	32.7	70.4	27.6
Pulaski	155	16.9	57.4									6.2	98.9	80.4	25.5	103.5	22.6
Rappahannock	157													95.7	24.3	95.7	24.3
Richmond	159													72.6	27.8	72.6	27.8
Roanoke	161									12.5	69.1	6.2	97.9	64.1	29.0	82.9	25.6
Rockbridge	163	60.6	30.9							18.7	56.4			174.7	17.5	254.1	14.4
Rockingham	165	151.7	19.0									6.0	99.7	135.8	19.8	293.5	13.4
Russell	167									11.4	70.0			134.4	20.4	145.9	19.5
Scott	169	45.6	35.5											202.9	16.3	248.5	14.8
Shenandoah	171	79.2	26.9											107.7	22.6	186.9	17.0
Smyth	173	73.7	28.2							10.6	72.4			99.9	23.3	184.2	17.3
Southampton	175													241.4	14.9	241.4	14.9
Spotsylvania	177									5.6	103.5	1.4	103.5	134.3	19.9	141.3	19.5
Stafford	179					17.6	58.3					5.6	103.5	103.4	22.3	126.5	20.3
Surry	181									1.3	107.5			141.8	19.9	143.1	19.7
Sussex	183													260.0	14.6	260.0	14.6
Tazewell	185	6.2	98.9									1.5	98.9	220.7	15.6	228.4	15.4
Warren	187							6.2	97.9	6.2	97.9			46.5	32.5	59.0	29.4
Washington	191	30.8	44.0							12.3	69.8	4.8	100.2	161.7	18.2	209.6	16.0
Westmoreland	193													82.6	25.3	82.6	25.3
Wise	195	12.2	70.4					8.1	77.2			6.2	98.9	146.8	18.8	159.0	18.1
Wythe	197	49.1	34.8					5.8	100.4	6.2	98.9			39.4	37.4	100.7	23.7
York	199					16.8	54.9					8.8	76.3	7.2	84.6	40.9	35.0
Chesapeake	550											3.5	98.6	32.0	42.2	41.3	36.5
Hampton	650													1.2	107.5	1.2	107.5
Newport News	700											5.9	100.4			5.9	100.4
Suffolk	800			5.9	100.4									141.2	19.7	147.1	19.3
Virginia Beach	810					3.9	107.5							31.3	42.0	35.2	39.2
All		1,638.7	5.0	5.9	100.4	132.2	20.3	93.3	24.1	271.6	14.2	194.7	16.5	12,906.7	1.1	15,243.2	0.8

FIPS = Federal Information Processing Standards; SE = sampling error.

Table C.17—Volume of live trees on timberland by county and major species group, Virginia, 2007

County	FIPS code	Unknown Volume (thousand cubic feet)	Unknown SE (percent)	Pine Volume (thousand cubic feet)	Pine SE (percent)	Other softwoods Volume (thousand cubic feet)	Other softwoods SE (percent)	Soft hardwoods Volume (thousand cubic feet)	Soft hardwoods SE (percent)	Hard hardwoods Volume (thousand cubic feet)	Hard hardwoods SE (percent)	Total Volume (thousand cubic feet)	Total SE (percent)
Accomack	1			221,052.2	30.1			61,151.5	31.1	58,095.0	29.9	340,298.8	26.3
Albemarle	3	147.7	103.5	73,667.0	30.4	12,133.1	58.6	205,644.5	22.8	319,215.1	18.1	610,807.4	15.8
Alleghany	5			68,004.4	28.3	4,390.2	80.6	48,695.1	43.3	261,843.6	18.3	382,933.3	17.3
Amelia	7			139,277.6	34.9	4,031.6	54.8	101,108.6	26.5	117,351.7	29.7	361,769.5	21.9
Amherst	9			82,808.8	30.6	5,128.7	49.5	158,774.0	22.2	185,691.8	21.9	432,403.2	17.7
Appomattox	11			28,329.5	39.2	1,738.5	62.3	71,721.8	36.4	79,212.3	28.6	181,002.1	23.8
Arlington	13												
Augusta	15			106,661.1	23.9	6,580.7	45.2	83,825.2	25.6	370,444.9	15.2	567,511.9	14.1
Bath	17			84,315.7	26.8	4,814.9	98.9	65,636.6	23.7	495,322.8	15.4	650,090.0	14.7
Bedford	19			81,787.8	34.6	2,658.3	40.6	241,842.4	19.8	304,131.9	18.5	630,420.5	15.1
Bland	21			29,888.4	40.1	16,777.8	79.4	88,649.6	34.9	238,807.5	20.8	374,123.3	21.8
Botetourt	23			50,905.6	35.4	5,595.6	42.4	124,765.8	28.2	227,439.2	18.7	408,706.2	18.1
Brunswick	25			241,134.4	25.1	1,051.8	50.2	119,705.5	27.4	107,112.4	31.4	469,004.2	20.0
Buchanan	27	63.0	98.9	7,203.1	95.1	14,403.0	51.5	267,695.8	20.9	350,427.6	18.3	639,792.5	16.0
Buckingham	29			163,644.1	24.5	6,009.5	76.5	109,483.1	25.6	225,504.6	18.4	504,641.4	15.4
Campbell	31			128,100.9	26.2	1,772.1	66.8	133,850.3	34.3	148,567.1	23.9	412,290.4	18.9
Caroline	33			177,986.7	23.5	341.4	51.0	186,435.0	30.7	210,802.5	22.4	575,565.6	18.3
Carroll	35			119,608.3	25.7	5,636.9	54.4	75,894.5	22.9	143,196.8	20.3	344,336.6	18.1
Charles City	36			115,428.0	37.9			86,527.3	39.3	58,304.3	40.2	260,259.5	28.1
Charlotte	37			122,081.2	30.5	2,182.4	54.9	129,621.8	34.9	97,681.8	30.1	351,567.2	22.1
Chesterfield	41			113,596.5	30.7	1,784.7	79.1	109,268.6	31.0	153,833.5	24.1	378,483.2	20.1
Clarke	43			279.6	97.9			16,229.4	52.5	50,630.7	53.8	67,139.7	52.5
Craig	45			40,864.8	27.8	42.3	99.7	24,542.4	47.6	188,359.5	22.5	253,809.0	21.1
Culpeper	47			39,467.3	63.4	5,066.3	74.9	81,392.8	36.7	111,732.9	30.4	237,659.2	25.8
Cumberland	49			104,268.6	31.8	766.7	61.1	47,293.7	33.6	68,406.3	36.0	220,735.3	25.3
Dickenson	51			6,520.3	67.6	6,326.5	50.3	139,604.9	21.8	235,337.4	21.3	387,789.0	18.4
Dinwiddie	53			149,712.3	28.2	2,501.0	63.3	111,106.9	24.4	114,419.9	25.7	377,740.1	19.9
Essex	57	145.0	107.5	60,432.8	38.5			40,182.0	36.3	25,208.9	44.7	125,968.7	29.4
Fairfax	59	382.7	96.6	4,092.9	89.8	2,133.8	75.8	77,695.4	31.3	183,181.9	31.6	267,486.8	27.8
Fauquier	61			24,757.8	38.7	8,631.3	46.7	132,709.9	29.5	257,269.8	20.2	423,368.9	18.7
Floyd	63	347.8	105.2	71,904.8	39.8	4,223.0	62.9	104,594.2	32.8	102,115.0	31.3	283,184.8	24.9
Fluvanna	65			28,405.6	35.0	747.7	70.9	39,153.8	31.1	94,203.5	29.2	162,510.6	24.1
Franklin	67			112,826.7	35.2	2,341.5	43.2	264,947.2	20.0	204,999.3	18.4	585,114.7	16.4
Frederick	69			39,881.5	36.9			32,830.0	32.3	258,545.1	21.6	331,256.6	20.4

continued

Table C.17—Volume of live trees on timberland by county and major species group, Virginia, 2007 (continued)

County	FIPS code	Unknown Volume thousand cubic feet	Unknown SE percent	Pine Volume thousand cubic feet	Pine SE percent	Other softwoods Volume thousand cubic feet	Other softwoods SE percent	Soft hardwoods Volume thousand cubic feet	Soft hardwoods SE percent	Hard hardwoods Volume thousand cubic feet	Hard hardwoods SE percent	Total Volume thousand cubic feet	Total SE percent
Giles	71			6,545.7	48.8	3,451.9	70.1	137,965.7	28.2	270,282.1	20.3	418,245.5	19.7
Gloucester	73			79,373.8	39.7			122,655.2	33.1	73,934.9	32.3	275,963.9	28.0
Goochland	75			75,236.0	40.0	1,408.9	47.4	104,347.0	40.1	104,459.7	36.4	285,451.6	26.1
Grayson	77			45,606.8	33.7	31,433.8	62.1	101,919.6	27.6	179,461.8	28.4	358,422.0	21.6
Greene	79			3,873.5	57.5	770.9	67.4	73,998.4	50.4	57,746.8	38.7	136,389.6	37.4
Greensville	81			112,340.3	34.4	410.7	107.5	79,569.5	31.0	79,601.9	29.0	271,922.5	25.6
Halifax	83			273,673.4	21.5	14,731.4	35.2	170,719.0	20.8	140,613.4	23.3	599,737.2	15.5
Hanover	85			128,915.0	23.6	656.8	46.1	159,254.4	25.4	169,091.1	25.6	457,917.3	19.2
Henrico	87			18,021.3	41.4	1,160.8	74.6	17,292.0	50.8	51,033.0	36.6	87,507.1	33.8
Henry	89			148,107.9	27.9	590.1	69.2	106,329.4	25.7	88,648.0	27.5	343,675.4	21.6
Highland	91			73,878.4	34.4	37,746.8	38.8	90,612.0	25.4	310,192.7	17.9	512,429.9	17.3
Isle of Wight	93			52,984.2	39.7	3,439.9	107.5	73,687.5	34.6	45,017.6	47.9	175,129.3	29.4
James City	95			35,362.4	47.1			43,210.3	44.9	74,012.4	36.9	152,585.1	34.2
King and Queen	97			65,384.3	31.1	207.7	70.9	88,589.4	38.7	82,277.5	30.2	236,458.9	24.5
King George	99			19,271.4	54.9	864.0	100.0	132,412.9	32.1	78,168.2	35.7	230,716.5	30.0
King William	101			74,773.2	37.5	862.6	86.7	80,833.9	34.2	47,721.2	38.7	204,190.9	27.3
Lancaster	103			33,512.2	49.1			23,055.4	41.4	28,822.5	49.5	85,390.1	38.9
Lee	105	174.9	100.2	4,275.7	72.4	12,221.7	44.8	142,667.1	23.4	255,815.7	22.1	415,155.1	20.9
Loudoun	107			5,658.7	65.1	10,807.0	60.9	80,826.8	32.7	194,993.7	24.3	292,286.1	22.1
Louisa	109			112,300.4	31.0	3,022.9	43.4	118,266.0	25.5	147,421.6	23.1	381,010.9	19.1
Lunenburg	111			180,518.3	27.2	1,308.4	48.7	130,970.8	23.7	123,192.1	23.7	435,989.6	19.3
Madison	113			35,575.0	68.6	104.8	96.6	66,103.1	48.4	104,469.0	43.9	206,251.9	35.1
Mathews	115			21,663.1	68.4			7,709.6	53.3	23,167.6	86.9	52,540.3	57.3
Mecklenburg	117			215,614.0	23.1	4,439.6	47.2	204,957.9	20.0	229,636.5	24.3	654,647.9	16.1
Middlesex	119			36,235.2	56.4			43,541.4	65.7	32,099.7	52.6	111,876.3	47.1
Montgomery	121			39,404.3	40.9	3,802.0	51.0	45,767.1	31.1	161,801.2	24.2	250,774.6	20.8
Nelson	125			63,640.4	36.7	4,992.0	66.2	219,320.5	22.5	283,996.3	18.3	571,949.2	16.3
New Kent	127			69,948.2	36.1	151.6	73.8	45,301.8	43.0	59,102.8	35.8	174,504.4	27.3
Northampton	131			47,189.6	61.3			15,267.1	89.9	3,701.0	85.2	66,157.7	59.1
Northumberland	133			26,689.7	73.2			45,395.8	38.2	49,148.9	39.9	121,234.4	34.9
Nottoway	135			90,393.5	36.4	1,342.0	65.1	59,519.5	29.4	70,748.5	33.5	222,003.5	25.0
Orange	137			21,871.1	46.3	10,592.0	66.8	139,665.5	29.5	156,663.6	29.7	328,792.2	24.5
Page	139	59.3	97.9	14,232.7	45.1	1,081.5	70.4	33,268.2	41.9	98,282.8	30.4	146,924.5	30.5
Patrick	141			48,077.6	35.7	157.6	100.3	214,042.4	23.4	189,156.3	21.6	451,434.0	19.2

continued

Table C.17—Volume of live trees on timberland by county and major species group, Virginia, 2007 (continued)

County	FIPS code	Unknown Volume (thousand cubic feet)	Unknown SE (percent)	Pine Volume (thousand cubic feet)	Pine SE (percent)	Other softwoods Volume (thousand cubic feet)	Other softwoods SE (percent)	Soft hardwoods Volume (thousand cubic feet)	Soft hardwoods SE (percent)	Hard hardwoods Volume (thousand cubic feet)	Hard hardwoods SE (percent)	Total Volume (thousand cubic feet)	Total SE (percent)
Pittsylvania	143			174,542.2	23.6	1,727.3	35.4	326,240.9	17.8	211,665.8	19.7	714,176.2	14.5
Powhatan	145			88,142.5	41.2	1,307.8	57.5	51,135.6	36.2	77,189.5	35.1	217,775.4	26.1
Prince Edward	147			74,798.6	30.6	1,996.0	44.7	54,057.1	33.4	57,876.1	41.5	188,727.8	25.0
Prince George	149			57,444.9	36.7	17,228.0	107.5	32,915.6	33.4	55,649.2	40.6	163,237.7	27.6
Prince William	153			36,946.2	49.6	1,544.7	51.0	59,527.9	39.8	122,946.8	34.5	220,965.6	30.0
Pulaski	155			31,945.3	31.2	685.4	84.0	31,271.3	37.1	132,648.0	26.4	196,549.9	24.2
Rappahannock	157			16,188.4	59.5	202.7	103.5	130,802.9	33.7	105,186.6	28.7	252,380.7	26.7
Richmond	159			53,889.7	47.0			52,169.1	35.2	45,214.2	38.7	151,273.0	31.7
Roanoke	161			28,558.3	37.2	240.9	83.4	39,085.5	53.8	78,331.7	30.7	146,216.3	28.4
Rockbridge	163			66,618.0	26.6	14,663.9	65.3	118,956.1	22.5	346,037.9	17.2	546,275.9	16.0
Rockingham	165	304.8	99.7	65,433.7	37.7	31,469.0	39.4	111,957.7	28.1	413,052.4	16.5	622,217.5	16.0
Russell	167			3,587.7	100.2	23,699.3	57.7	145,454.3	28.8	184,637.1	22.4	357,378.3	21.5
Scott	169			13,167.5	42.5	18,635.1	47.2	247,511.1	22.6	339,610.9	19.6	618,924.6	17.9
Shenandoah	171			17,755.4	34.3	235.7	70.3	60,223.0	31.7	271,096.6	20.0	349,310.7	19.4
Smyth	173			15,001.1	48.2	8,169.4	51.6	130,849.4	30.3	240,580.1	21.5	394,600.0	22.4
Southampton	175			204,208.2	23.1	8,596.1	56.0	141,779.4	24.6	90,211.6	34.4	444,795.2	19.0
Spotsylvania	177			124,673.5	33.0	1,692.9	77.5	133,340.8	28.6	123,673.2	27.2	383,380.3	22.8
Stafford	179			18,764.7	49.1	911.6	81.2	145,154.9	26.9	204,352.5	25.7	369,183.7	22.1
Surry	181			106,517.8	28.1	56.9	107.5	81,007.5	37.4	47,156.4	43.9	234,738.6	24.5
Sussex	183			220,137.8	27.8	490.7	89.6	72,808.5	30.1	75,366.9	31.1	368,803.8	22.3
Tazewell	185			3,230.8	54.0	823.2	87.0	161,548.1	24.3	276,502.4	18.7	442,104.4	17.9
Warren	187			15,390.3	62.3	533.3	79.6	29,892.7	53.8	96,730.9	35.8	142,547.2	32.0
Washington	191			21,765.0	40.9	18,920.9	75.4	190,728.9	20.3	296,277.5	20.7	527,692.3	18.2
Westmoreland	193			27,080.5	46.0			85,306.7	37.4	72,218.9	40.2	184,606.1	32.0
Wise	195			6,262.4	56.8	9,335.6	58.9	155,698.6	27.7	111,396.1	27.4	282,692.6	23.5
Wythe	197	200.6	100.2	27,365.5	34.9	1,016.3	88.3	15,698.9	41.7	118,079.7	30.3	162,361.0	27.3
York	199			39,011.9	43.4			65,698.9	55.6	60,582.7	47.4	165,293.5	40.5
Chesapeake	550			54,161.9	47.5			37,404.0	50.1	9,545.7	53.1	101,111.6	43.0
Hampton	650			4,817.2	107.5			4,100.0	107.5	578.3	107.5	9,495.4	107.5
Newport News	700			12,766.4	100.4			2,542.1	100.4	1,598.2	100.4	16,906.8	100.4
Suffolk	800			154,176.5	28.8	18,334.5	97.7	101,366.4	32.6	35,830.9	37.6	309,708.3	25.2
Virginia Beach	810			37,336.2	71.7	3,755.9	96.3	49,698.5	48.8	7,032.6	72.8	97,823.2	44.0
All		1,825.9	38.3	6,940,730.0	3.4	467,843.8	11.0	9,867,553.7	2.7	14,420,736.3	1.9	31,698,689.7	1.4

FIPS = Federal Information Processing Standards; SE = sampling error.

77

Rose, Anita K. 2009. Virginia's forests, 2007. Resour. Bull. SRS–159. Asheville, NC: U.S.
    Department of Agriculture Forest Service, Southern Research Station. 77 p.

Between 2002 and 2007, the Forest Service's Forest Inventory and Analysis (FIA) Program
conducted the eighth inventory of the forests of Virginia. About 15.7 million acres, or 62
percent, of Virginia was forested. The majority (12.4 million acres) of Virginia's forest land was
in nonindustrial private forest ownership. Public ownership and forest industry ranked second
and third, with 2.8 and 0.6 million acres, respectively. Red maple dominated the number of
live stems (≥ 1.0 inch d.b.h.) with 1.4 billion stems (13 percent of total). Loblolly pine was
second, with 1.0 billion live stems. While yellow-poplar was the most dominate species for
live-tree volume with 5.0 billion cubic feet (15 percent of total), as a genus, oaks accounted
for 33 percent of the live-tree volume (10.8 billion cubic feet). Biomass of coarse woody debris
on forest health plots averaged 2.9 tons per acre for the State. The amount of carbon in coarse
woody debris and fine woody debris averaged 1.4 and 1.7 tons per acre, respectively. The Forest
Service's FIA is the only program that conducts forest assessments across all land in the United
States. Increasing demands on the resource and anthropogenic-related impacts on forests have
intensified the need to conduct ecosystem-based inventories such as these.

Keywords: FIA, forest health, forest inventory, forest land, forest survey, timberland, Virginia.

July 2009

Southern Research Station
200 W.T. Weaver Blvd.
Asheville, NC 28804

Commonwealth of Virginia:
Old Dominion State

Capital City: Richmond

Location: 37.53105 N, 077.47458 W

Origin of State's Name: Named for England's "Virgin Queen," Elizabeth I

Nicknames: Old Dominion, Mother of Presidents

Population: 7,078,515

Geology: Land Area; 39,594 sq. mi.

Highest Point: Mt. Rogers; 5,729 feet

Inland Water: 1,063 sq. mi.

Largest City: Virginia Beach

Lowest Point: Atlantic coast; sea level

Border States: Kentucky - Maryland - North Carolina - Tennessee - West Virginia

Coastline: 112 mi.

Constitution: 10th State

Statehood: June 25, 1788

Motto: Sic Semper Tyrannis - Thus Always to Tyrants

Bird: In 1950, the General Assembly chose the northern cardinal *(Cardinalis cardinalis)* as the State bird because of its bright plumage and cheerful song. In eighteenth-century England, the cardinal was called "the Virginia nightingale." The cardinal is part of the finch family.

Agriculture: Cattle, poultry, dairy products, tobacco, hogs, soybeans, apples, potatoes, tomatoes, peanuts.

Industry: Transportation equipment, textiles, food processing, printing, electric equipment, chemicals.

Minerals: Virginia is one of the top ten coal producers in the U.S. Coal accounts for about 70 percent of Virginia's mineral value; crushed stone and gravel, lime, and kyanite are also mined.

Flag: In 1861, the Virginia State Convention passed an ordinance establishing a design virtually identical to that in current use. This flag has a deep blue field with a circular white center. The obverse of the great seal of the Commonwealth has been identically painted or embroidered on each side of the flag. A white silk fringe adorns the edge farthest from the flag staff.

Tree: In 1956, the State adopted the American dogwood *(Cornus florida)* as the official tree. The dogwood is well distributed throughout the Commonwealth, and its beauty is symbolic of the many attractive features of Virginia. The dogwood blooms in early spring and its blossom is a tiny cluster of flowers surrounded by four white leaves that look like petals.

Flower: In 1918, the State floral emblem commonly known as the American dogwood was adopted. It was selected to foster a feeling of pride in our State and to stimulate an interest in the history and traditions of the Commonwealth.

Presidential Birthplace:

George Washington, 1789-1797
Thomas Jefferson, 1801-1809
James Madison, 1809-1817
James Monroe, 1817-1825
William Henry Harrison, 1841
John Tyler, 1841-1845
Zachary Taylor, 1849-1850
Woodrow Wilson, 1913-1921

Seal: The great seal of the Commonwealth was adopted by the Virginia's Constitutional Convention on July 5, 1776. Its design was the work of a committee composed of George Mason, George Wythe, Richard Henry Lee, and Robert Carter Nicholas. George Wythe was probably the principal designer, taking its theme from ancient Roman mythology.

The original design was never properly cast and a number of variations came into use. Attempting to legislate uniformity, the General Assemblies of 1873 and 1903 passed acts describing the seal in detail. In 1930, a committee was named to prepare an "accurate and faithful description of the great seal of the Commonwealth, as it was intended to be by Mason and Wythe and their associates." The committee set forth the official design in use today, which is essentially the design adopted by the Virginia's Constitutional Convention of 1776.

Official colors were established by the Art Commission in 1949 and a water color, the only official model for flag makers and stationers, hangs in the office of the Secretary of the Commonwealth. The Secretary of the Commonwealth is designated by the Code of Virginia as the keeper of the great seal. The great seal of the Commonwealth is affixed to documents signed by the governor and intended for use before tribunals and for purposes outside the jurisdiction of Virginia.